THE TROUBLED TUMMY COOKBOOK

JUNE ROTH

Foreword by Harold L. Scales, M.D.

cbi Contemporary Books, Inc.
Chicago

To Susanna and Johan, who give me
indescribable pride and joy.

Sincere and grateful thanks for information and guidance go to Dr. Dorothy Rathman, Best Foods nutritionist, and to Helen Purnhagen, chief dietician of Englewood Hospital, Englewood, New Jersey.

Contents

Foreword

The Troubled Tummy Cookbook accepts the challenge to eliminate the bland-diet blahs. The patient's lot has always been a hard one: no one in the past has had the imagination or motivation to offer palatable and tasty recipes for the various sick-stomach diets.

June Roth takes us effortlessly and painlessly on a cook's tour down the alimentary tract, from ingestion to elimination. With the clarity of a nonmedical writer, she explains the physiology of digestion so that all of us can understand and then proceeds to detail recipes that keep our systems working well.

Why do patients have to suffer the tasteless, unappetizing diets prescribed by doctors for gastrointestinal malaise? There is a better way, and June Roth shows it to us here. With full awareness of the growth of knowledge and understanding of gastrointestinal disease, she offers us both the traditional diets and alternatives more recently in vogue, all with redeemingly good taste.

Ulcer patients have traditionally followed a whole milk and cream regime, but June Roth realizes that a special diet doesn't help at all if it kills them with a coronary because we've loaded them with cholesterol. Her diet uses skimmed or defatted milk.

She respects our health and protects us from obesity by watching calories—they do count, even in special diets. She understands the need to balance a diet with the proper proportions of carbohydrate, protein, and fat to ensure good nutrition. Supplements of vitamins, iron, and other minerals, if needed, should be prescribed by your doctor.

These diets also consider the new approach to constipation and chronic diverticulitis: eating the bulk lacking in traditional bland diets. June Roth has admirably translated medically sound principles, founded on good clinical judgment, and the experience of gastroenterologists and physiologists, into practicable eating programs. She gives us recipes that make drab and restricted diets tolerable—and even outright enjoyable.

Certainly, as a doctor, I unqualifiedly recommend this book to my patients.

Harold L. Scales, M.D., F.A.C.P., F.C.C.P.

Dear Reader:

Whenever a special diet is recommended by your doctor for a troubled tummy in your household, you need help—and you'll find positive help in this book. You'll find lists of foods allowed and foods not allowed in each diet category, followed by sample meal plans. Each section has its own recipes to help you follow your doctor's orders—and still enjoy eating.

Each section also includes a list of recipes from other sections that can be used for the prescribed diet—don't interchange recipes from other categories unless they appear on this list. The differences are subtle, and other recipes might seem to be suitable, but only the listed recipes are medically advised for each diet.

Patients and their families are often upset when they're faced with a special diet, because no one has interpreted the directions for them, no one has actually showed them recipes that taste good and follow the prescribed diet. This cookbook has been a labor of caring on my part, an effort to fill that need and to ease the burden of carrying out the necessary restrictions. It will help you eat with a minimum of fuss and a maximum of satisfaction.

I can't say that following a specialized diet is easy for the family cook, but it is possible to avoid slipping back into harmful eating habits, and this book shows you the way. With proper preventive measures and your doctor's care, it should help you eat your way back to good health.

Sincerely,

June Roth

1

Soothing Words for the Cook

Something in your digestive tract is causing a ruckus, and your doctor has prescribed a special diet. Perhaps it's a temporary measure, perhaps a permanent regime. Either way, you have to understand the restrictions and then adapt them to palatable food. The better your meals taste, the easier it is to adhere to the diet and not be tempted to cheat. The more closely you follow the diet, the less likely it is that you'll have flareups of whatever sensitive spot is creating the problem.

The major difficulty with special diets is that they can cause chaos in the kitchen; it's hard to prepare special meals for just one person. There are several ways to get around this. One is to try to devise recipes that will meet the needs of the patient and be well received by the rest of the family too. Another is to tape a list of dos and don'ts to the inside of a kitchen cabinet door for easy referral. And the most important way is to plan menus for several days in advance, so the necessary ingredients are always on hand when mealtime approaches.

Don't be embarrassed to question your doctor or dietician at great length to be sure you understand all the restrictions and directions. Study the lists you receive and jot down ideas of how

1

best to follow them, making notes of what favorite foods will have to be eliminated and what possible substitutions you can make for them. And remember, special diets were never intended as a punishment, either for the patient or for the cook. They're simply a part of the medical treatment you need for controlled comfort or for recovery.

Frequently, you'll find it necessary to change the style of your cooking. If you've been depending on convenience foods for a head start, you'll have to learn how to read labels very carefully to be sure that no restricted foods are on the list of ingredients. As you reach for the old-time flavoring standbys of onions, salt, pepper, herbs, and spices, you'll have to check the list to see whether they're permitted.

Methods of cooking may need a vital changeover too. If you're used to frying and roasting, you may have to learn the techniques of broiling, braising, and poaching. The seriousness with which you follow the cooking rules of your diet will be reflected in your improved well-being.

Troubled tummies, however minor the cause, can upset an entire household; many patients crankily resent the imposition made by the frailty of the human body. When the cause is chronic, and your patient unhappy and uncomfortable, you'll have to make a greater effort to present food in the most attractive ways. It's helpful to follow the hospital method of presenting small portions on many plates to help to create the illusion of fine dining. And this is the time to use your nicest china, colorful placemats, a flower in a bud vase, and any other cheerful accessory you may have to enhance the meal. Try to present a treat instead of a treatment, to minimize the change of food habits.

Of course, it's easier to accomplish these goals in your own home than to do so in restaurants and as a guest in other homes. Get a few menus of restaurants where you eat often and go over the possibilities. Learn how to order to get the food you want and still follow your diet; or help your patient do the same.

When you're in a restaurant, don't hesitate to say that you want something broiled instead of fried, no salt, no butter, or whatever, if you know that the dish can be made to order. Don't expect prepared soups and vegetables to be salt-free, and don't expect spices to be omitted from sauces that have been simmering for hours. By studying the menus at home, you can practice how to order away from home, reducing any tension or embarrassment that could spoil an adventure in a restaurant.

When you or your patient get invitations to other homes, accept with an explanation of what accommodations will have to be made so you can attend the dinner. If the hostess is planning too many things that don't fit your diet, and you realize that it would be an imposition to have a special meal prepared, don't hesitate to say that you'll bring one dinner with you. Then plan it carefully, so you don't have to clutter up your host and hostess's kitchen with too many of your pots and pans. Perhaps you can assemble the dinner in an aluminum TV dinner tray, to be reheated and spooned onto a china plate. If you keep the fuss to a minimum, you'll dine comfortably with the other guests, and no mention need be made of diet restrictions.

The most helpful thing you can do, for yourself or for someone else who has a digestive tract problem, is to accept dietary regulations with whole-hearted grace. This book will help you cope with the limitations with as much ease and enjoyment as possible.

2

Little Troubles/
Big Troubles

The human digestive system is so complicated it's a wonder everyone doesn't have something out of whack. In fact, at one time or another, many people do suffer from some discomfort, whether caused by a dysfunction of one of our hard-working organs or by allergies, ulcers, heartburn, nausea, gastritis, constipation, diarrhea, ileitis, or any of an assortment of other possible breakdowns in the miraculously designed food-processing machine that runs through each of us.

From the time we swallow food, it is mashed and shredded into tiny particles that are bathed with chemicals to separate the nutrients from the waste. As the processed foodstuff is pushed along, cells along the digestive tract absorb only the nutrients needed to keep the body going. The rest travels on through the alimentary canal from mouth to anus.

Applying Murphy's Law—If anything can go wrong, invariably it will—someday you or someone in your household will suffer from a troubled tummy. Usually you can learn all the possible miseries and solutions from others who are anxious to share the burden of their woes. In case you've missed hearing about a few twists and turns that parts of the digestive tract can spring on unsuspecting host bodies, let's follow the route of possibilities, and of food prescriptions to ease the pain they can cause. All these ailments may even make you happier about coping with the one killjoy that's causing problems for you.

Remember that a layman cannot and should not attempt to diagnose and treat *any* pain or change of bowel habits. Take the problem to a competent medical doctor who will test for serious origins of distress and prescribe the proper medication and diet. This book is intended to augment the doctor's directions, to give suitable recipes for every kind of diet restriction, and to help you ask pertinent questions of your doctor so that even the limited foods prescribed can be prepared in a tasty manner.

If you or your patient has been hospitalized, don't hesitate to seek special diet help from the head dietician of the hospital. Diet manuals vary from one hospital to another, but most agree on basic special diets, including or omitting a few fringe foods. If those foods are important to you, ask specifically whether they can be included. Just be sure not to pester for foods that are obviously out of range, because your pity for your own or your patient's taste buds can cause real pain for a tummy on the rampage.

You'll be able to communicate better with your doctor if you understand in general terms how the human digestive system works.

The Mouth

From the moment the *mouth* opens and accepts food, the entire digestive mechanism swings into action. Teeth grind the food into small particles and the *salivary glands*—the *parotid* glands in front of the ears, the *sublingual* glands under the tongue, and the *submandibular* glands under the lower jaw—release enough saliva to moisten and soften the particles so they easily slide down the *esophagus*.

Some people have chronic increases or decreases from the normal quart to quart and a half of saliva secretions a day. Either abnormality can be caused by extreme nervous tension, and either can be a mischief-maker to the digestive tract. Since saliva not only moistens food but also provides enzymes for digesting starch, it's important to chew starchy food well to mix enough saliva through it. Intestinal gas is often caused by a poor breakdown of starches in the mouth and resultant digestion problems.

The Esophagus

The esophagus is the swallowing mechanism that drops the food mass through its muscular tube, kneading it downward into the *stomach* with a pushing-squeezing process called *peristalsis*. Liquids flow through the esophagus in about a second, while chewed food takes about seven seconds to reach the stomach.

The esophagus can have congenital defects, outpocketings, inflammations, strictures, tumors, or ulcers. *Esophagitis*, a chronic condition, is sometimes caused by a repeated regurgitation of gastric acid from the stomach back up into the esophagus; in these cases, alcoholic beverages, the use of tobacco, and certain irritating foods and spices can make matters worse. Your doctor will take medical steps to relieve the condition and will often recommend a *bland diet* as part of the treatment.

Hiatus Hernia

When part of the stomach protrudes up into or next to the esophagus, it is called a *hiatus hernia*. It can cause pain, burning sensations, or regurgitation. Obese patients are generally advised to follow a *weight-reduction diet*; comfort can also be obtained from antacids, and by propping up the patient with several extra pillows when in bed. Sometimes surgery is necessary to bring relief.

The Stomach

The esophagus connects directly to the stomach, which is located behind the lower ribs. The stomach is a rather shapeless pouch, something like a baggy curved gourd, with its

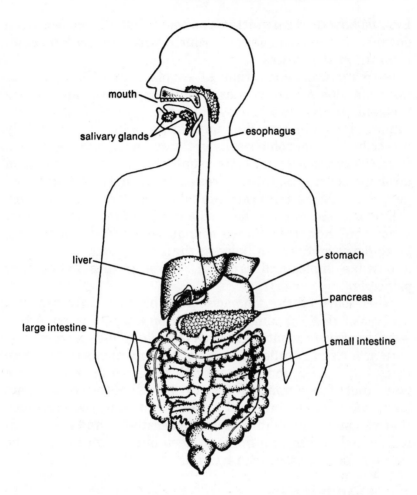

fat end at the top and its lower stem leading into the slender tube of the *duodenum*. When it's empty, it hangs in a saggy formless mass, and when full it plumps out.

The stomach can hold about two quarts of food at a time. Normally, it takes about three hours to process a meal and empty it into the duodenum through a sphincter known as the *pylorus*. As the pylorus expands and contracts, it pushes small amounts of bulk, now called *chyme*, through to the duodenum.

Liquids flow through quickly and easily, but all food is broken down with stomach *enzymes*, which, with *hydrochloric acid*, form the *gastric juices*.

With all the action that takes place in this organ, it's understandable that it occasionally bogs down and causes problems, such as heartburn, indigestion, gastritis, ulcers, and tumors. Depending on the diagnosis, a bland diet is usually prescribed, either temporarily or for extended periods of time. In addition, stomach patients usually have to avoid the use of alcoholic beverages, tobacco, coffee, irritating seasonings like pepper, and irritating foods like cabbage, turnips, and onions.

Doctors used to prescribe frequent sips of milk or cream for ulcers, but now many have acknowledged that the staying protein power of skim milk meets the same need while avoiding a possible cholesterol problem. These recipes follow that principle.

When part of the stomach must be surgically removed because of ulcers or tumors, a *gastrectomy* is performed. Afterward, to prevent what is known as the *dumping syndrome*, the patient is usually ordered to eat many tiny meals rather than three large ones, and to avoid rich foods while staying on a bland diet. The stomach eventually stretches to accommodate larger meals again, but until it does, it is usually recommended that you stay on a high-protein, moderate-fat, and low-starch regime, while limiting fluids to keep bulk down to what the smaller-sized stomach can handle.

The Small Intestine

The first ten inches or so of the small intestine is called the duodenum. This is a busy little section of the approximately twenty-two-foot-long small intestine that lies all wound up in the abdomen. The duodenum is a tight little C-shaped tube, connected on one side to the stomach, where the pyloris pushes acid-bathed nutrients into it, and on the other side to the *jejunum*.

Tiny though it may be, the duodenum is the focal point where digestion and absorption take place. It is an alkaline area, in contrast to the acid area of the stomach, and is connected to ducts bringing bile from the *liver* and fluid from the nearby *pancreas*. It's also a common area for ulcers to occur. When they do, a bland diet is usually prescribed and the elimination of pepper, spicy food, alcoholic beverages, coffee, and tobacco is recommended.

The duodenum connects with the ten-foot-long jejunum, which in turn connects with the ten- to twelve-foot-long *ileum*, with all three sections constituting the small intestine. It takes about ten hours for chyme to pass through the small intestine. The intestine is lined with a dense carpet of millions of projecting *villi*, which agitate the semiliquid mass and then absorb the digested elements of the carbohydrates and proteins, passing them on to a network of blood vessels to carry nutrition throughout the body.

Assimilated fats are mostly passed into *lymph* channels, and into the main bloodstream. The waste product, chyme, is pushed on into the *large intestine* through the narrow tube of the ileum into the wider tube of the *cecum*. By the way, in case you've ever wondered exactly where the appendix is, it dangles from the cecum, on the lower right hand side of the body.

A strict bland diet is usually recommended for problems in the small intestine. These range from diverticula or out-pouchings, ulcers, obstructions, and acute inflammation of the ileum to an inflammatory disease known as *regional enteritis*, which can occur in the ileum and jejunum.

Sometimes trouble is caused by a malabsorption syndrome, particularly the sprue syndrome known in children as *celiac disease*. Patients are usually told to follow a *gluten-free diet* that eliminates wheat and rye altogether.

The Large Intestine
The large intestine has the shape of a huge question mark, with chyme entering at the bottom of the curve, going upward to the ribs, crossing the body, and then curving down to the *rectum* to exit through the anus. It's a wider tube than the small in-

testine, but only about five feet long. It has a strong muscle at its opening to prevent chyme from backing up into the small intestine.

The five-foot-long large intestine has no villi lining its walls, and this slows the movement of the chyme. It takes about thirteen hours for the chyme to pass through the large intestine, and as it gradually loses its watery state it becomes fecal matter, made up of the residue of undigested food, cells shed from the intestinal lining, digestive secretions, and a great deal of bacteria. Most of the liquid has left the fecal bulk and it leaves the body in compact form through the rectum and finally through the anus.

Troubles in the large intestine, or the *colon* as it is often called, include colitis, constipation, diarrhea, functional disturbances, and diverticulosis, or outpouchings. Diet treatments differ for each of these.

Colitis generally requires a bland diet and at times a soft diet, along with the proper medication to calm the colon when it overreacts to certain foods and to emotional stresses.

Constipation, which is an extreme hardening of the fecal matter, can be overcome by including prunes, dates, raisins, bran cereals, and leafy vegetables. A *high-residue diet* will help in chronic cases.

Diarrhea can be of little or of great significance as a symptom of a more serious situation. Since the body loses a good deal of fluid, potassium, and sodium during an attack of diarrhea, it's important to replace the lost elements. Generally a *liquid diet* is advised, with salted broth, skim milk, and whatever medications have been prescribed to make up for the body losses. The first solid foods may be rice and bananas; then a soft diet or a bland diet may be prescribed.

Diverticulosis is caused by a series of outpouchings along the intestinal tract. The important thing is to keep those pouches from becoming inflamed, and possibly bursting. Doctors usually recommend avoiding food with pits, like raw tomatoes, and any other possible irritants. Some doctors recommend a bland diet while others recommend a high-residue diet to keep the bowel functioning smoothly. An attack of diverticulitis is often confused with an attack of appendicitis, so it's a good idea to keep both possibilities in mind when similar symptoms appear.

The Liver

While the *liver* is not part of the basic alimentary canal, it's an important organ of digestion. It weighs about four pounds and is located in the upper part of the abdomen, mostly on the right side of the body. Besides breaking down food molecules for the body, it also produces *bile*, which flows into the duodenum to aid digestive operations there. It also detoxifies poisons, manufactures cholesterol, and stores glycogen, which it has converted from glucose.

The liver can be afflicted with jaundice, a disease of excess bile in the circulatory system; cirrhosis, an inflammation frequently caused by alcoholism and poor nutrition; infectious hepatitis; and tumors. All are serious troubles and require good medical attention. A *low-fat diet* may be prescribed if there's difficulty in digesting a fatty meal, or a *low-sodium diet* if the condition has produced edema, a swelling of the legs.

The Gallbladder

The *gallbladder* is a three-inch-long sac attached to the underside of the liver. Its function is to store excess bile, modifying it chemically to concentrate and squeeze into the duodenum as needed. Sometimes the gallbladder becomes inflamed because of a bacterial infection, and sometimes it becomes inflamed because gallstones have formed, which can block the bile duct.

Usually doctors prescribe a low-fat diet for an inflamed gallbladder to prevent painful attacks caused by fatty meals. Frequent attacks can be resolved by the removal of the gallbladder, an operation called a *cholecystectomy*, as this tiny organ can be spared from the body if necessary. Sometimes a *postcholecystectomy syndrome* occurs after the gallbladder removal, where fatty foods still can't be tolerated, and in this event the patient will have to stay on a low-fat diet for life.

When Trouble Strikes

There's a saying in the medical world that only a fool tries to diagnose his own affliction. When symptoms like pain, nausea, vomiting, diarrhea, constipation, abdominal swelling, or dizziness occur, get a competent diagnosis from a doctor. If special diet instructions are given, be sure you understand exactly how to follow them.

The specialized diets in this book should be of considerable help to you in planning menus. Recipes are included for each diet restriction to help you prepare tasty meals as you learn how to adapt your kitchen to the recommended regime. It's no fun when food gets dull, and many times it's not necessary even when the meal must be salt-free, sugar-free, soft, or bland. It's amazing how quickly you or your patient can adjust to a special diet when your food is prepared well and presented attractively.

Most of the recipes in this book will appeal to the entire family, even though they're geared to the patient in your household. If you prefer to keep special diet meals separate, you can prepare them and then freeze the extra portions. The best way to do this is with boil-in-the-bag equipment, currently available in most large department stores.

This equipment consists of an electric sealer that makes special plastic bags air-tight. These can be safely frozen and then dropped into boiling water for quick reheating. If you seal one portion into each bag, you'll soon have a freezer bank of special diet dishes for your patient. Even without this equipment, extra portions can be frozen in air-tight individual containers and then reheated in the top of a double boiler over water, or in the oven. Even a small freezer compartment in your refrigerator is helpful in keeping meals varied and reducing time in the kitchen.

The better prepared you are to cope with a special diet, the more likely it is that you'll be able to follow it. Doctors and medications can't do it alone when special diets are part of the preventive medicine or convalescent regime. Your diet may or may not be a matter of life and death, but it's often a matter of comfort and recovery. This book will help you do a good job of it.

3

Liquid Diets

The Clear Liquid Diet

The clear liquid diet is prescribed when it is necessary to limit the amount of undigested food matter in the gastrointestinal tract. This can be done by serving your patient only clear broths, strained juices, tea, black coffee, and carbonated beverages. The only solid foods allowed are fruit-flavored gelatin and ices, as both liquefy at body temperature.

The important thing about this diet is to make sure your patient eats at least six times a day, to prevent dehydration. Because the diet is so extreme, it should be used only for short periods of time. If the patient must be kept on this regime for an extended time, your doctor may order vitamin supplements.

14

	FOODS ALLOWED	**FOODS TO OMIT**
Beverages:	Tea with lemon and sugar, coffee with sugar, carbonated beverages.	Milk, cream, all others.
Vegetables·	Tomato juice.	All others.
Fruit:	Strained lemonade, apple juice.	All others.
Soup:	Clear broth, clear bouillon.	All others.
Dessert:	Fruit-flavored gelatin, fruit ices.	All others.
Miscellaneous:	Sugar, plain hard sugar candy, salt, spices.	All others.

SUGGESTED MENU PLAN

Breakfast
Fruit juice
Beverage

Mid-morning
Fruit-flavored gelatin

Lunch
Broth
Fruit-flavored gelatin
Beverage

Mid-afternoon
Fruit juice
Fruit ices

Dinner
Broth
Fruit-flavored gelatin

Bedtime
Fruit juice

The Full Liquid Diet

The full liquid diet is prescribed when your patient can't tolerate solid foods but can manage to eat some strained foods. These patients can also digest milk products, so food may be creamed as directed. Bonus desserts include custards, gelatin, ices, sherbets, and plain ice cream—all of which liquefy at body temperature.

With careful menu planning, you can get a good balance of nutrients in the six meals indicated in the suggested menu plan. High protein levels can be maintained by following the directions for preparing the allowed meats, serving eggnogs, and using milk in custards and cream soups.

This type of diet can be satisfactory for short periods of time. For a longer regime, your doctor may order vitamin supplements.

	FOODS ALLOWED	FOODS TO OMIT
Beverages:	All milk beverages —include 2 to 6 cups daily. Tea, coffee, cocoa; carbonated beverages.	All others.
Eggs:	Mixed in beverage, such as eggnog; soft custard.	All cooked eggs.
Fats:	Light or heavy cream, butter or margarine (used in soup or cereal).	All others.
Breads and cereals:	Strained cereal— include at least once daily.	All others.

Vegetables:	Tomato juice; cooked and pureed —asparagus, string beans, wax beans, celery, carrots, potatoes, spinach, and tomatoes— may be stirred into cream soups.	All others.
Fruit:	Strained fruit juices.	All others.
Soup:	Clear broth, clear bouillon, strained cream soups.	All others.
Meat, fish, and poultry:	Cooked and finely homogenized, stirred into allowed soup. Liver— especially recommended.	All others.
Desserts:	Fruit-flavored gelatin; soft custard; rennet desserts, such as junket; fruit ices, plain sherbet, plain ice cream.	All others; be sure none of the allowed foods has seeds, nuts, or fruit added.
Miscellaneous:	Salt, spices, sugar, plain hard sugar candy.	All others.

SUGGESTED MENU PLAN

Breakfast
Citrus juice
Strained cereal, with
milk, sugar, and butter
Hot beverage

Mid-morning
Milk or eggnog

Lunch
Juice
Strained soup
Dessert
Milk
Hot beverage

Mid-afternoon
Milk or eggnog

Dinner
Juice
Strained soup
Dessert
Milk
Hot beverage

Bedtime
Milk or eggnog

RECIPES

In addition to these recipes for a Full Liquid Diet, the following recipes may also be used:

Beverages:
    Double Milk Eggnog 54
    Slim Skimnog 54

Soup:
    Chicken Broth (strained) 33
    Beef Bouillon (strained) 33
    Strained Cream Soup #1   56

Eggnog

1 egg
1 teaspoon sugar
1 cup milk
1 teaspoon vanilla

Break the egg into an electric blender. Add sugar and blend. Add milk and vanilla. Blend well. Makes about 1¼ cups.

NOTE: If electric blender is not available, use electric or hand beater. A variety of flavors can be obtained by substituting 1 tablespoon of chocolate syrup, 1 teaspoon instant coffee, or 1 teaspoon of other extract flavors for the vanilla. If desired, a dash of nutmeg may be added to the vanilla eggnog.

Orange Eggnog

1 egg
1 cup orange juice
2 teaspoons honey

Break the egg into an electric blender. Blend. Add orange juice and honey. Blend well. Makes about 1¼ cups.

NOTE: If electric blender is not available, use electric or hand beater and then pour through a fine strainer.

Strained Cereal

1 cup water
¼ teaspoon salt
2 tablespoons farina, cream of wheat, or oatmeal
½ cup milk
1 teaspoon butter
½ teaspoon sugar or brown sugar

Combine water and salt in the top of a double boiler; bring to a boil. At the same time, bring some water to a boil in the bottom of the double boiler. Stir cereal into the boiling salted water and place top of double boiler over simmering water in lower pan. Cook and stir until cereal is of a thin consistency, about 8 minutes. Press cereal through a strainer, or process on high in an electric blender. Add milk, butter, and sugar; reheat if necessary. Makes 1 serving.

Pureed Vegetables for Creamed Soup

METHOD #1: Place ½ cup canned or cooked vegetables in an electric blender. Add ½ cup of the cooking liquid. Blend until mixture is a fine thick sauce.

METHOD #2: Place ½ cup canned or cooked vegetables in a food mill. Add ½ cup of the cooking liquid. Force through the food mill.

METHOD #3: Place ½ cup canned or cooked vegetables in a fine strainer. Add ½ cup of the cooking liquid. Force through the strainer, using the back of a wooden spoon.

NOTE· Blended tomatoes must be strained to remove seeds. These pureed vegetables must be mixed with a creamed soup to be served as part of the full liquid diet.

Creamed Soup for Pureed Vegetables

2 **cups milk**
2 **tablespoons butter**
2 **tablespoons flour**
½ **teaspoon salt**
1 **cup pureed vegetables**

Heat milk in a saucepan. In another saucepan, melt butter; stir in flour and cook until mixture thickens. Gradually stir hot milk into the thickened mixture, stirring constantly. Add salt and pureed vegetables. Makes 3 servings.

Cream of Chicken Soup

2 **tablespoons butter**
2 **tablespoons flour**
2 **cups hot chicken broth**
Salt and pepper to taste

Melt butter in a saucepan; stir in flour and cook until mixture thickens. Gradually pour in hot chicken broth, stirring constantly until mixture thickens. Season with salt and pepper as desired. Makes 3 servings.

Soft Custard

2 cups milk
3 eggs, beaten
2 tablespoons sugar
1 teaspoon vanilla

Pour ½ cup milk into beaten eggs; add sugar and vanilla and beat until thick. Scald the remaining 1½ cups milk; add egg mixture and continue to cook and stir until mixture thickens. Do not bring to boiling, as mixture may curdle. Pour into custard cups and cool; chill until ready to serve. Makes 6 servings.

Lemon Ice

½ envelope (1½ teaspoons) unflavored gelatin
½ cup sugar
¾ cup water
3 egg whites
½ cup strained lemon juice

Combine gelatin and ¼ cup sugar in a saucepan. Blend in water, stirring until smooth. Bring mixture to a boil, stirring until gelatin is dissolved. Remove from heat. Beat egg whites at high speed until soft peaks form; add remaining sugar gradually, continuing to beat until all sugar is used and whites are stiff, but not dry. Continue beating, adding the warm mixture in a thin steady stream. Beat in lemon juice. Pour into two ice cube trays and freeze until mushy, stirring once or twice. When mixture is evenly frozen to the mushy stage, transfer to a chilled mixing bowl. With chilled beaters, beat at high speed until smooth and light. Return to freezer until firm. Makes 8 servings.

4

The Soft Diet

The soft diet is prescribed when the patient must restrict indigestible carbohydrates and omit meats or shellfish with tough connective tissue that's hard to digest. When the patient has a chewing difficulty, this diet may have to be served in minced or pureed form.

A large variety of foods is allowed in this diet, so careful menu planning can allow a nutritionally adequate diet without additional vitamin supplements. The main problem for the cook is thinking up ways to make the soft-textured foods look appetizing to the patient. This can be accomplished by selecting foods of different colors, giving each meal enough eye-appeal to make up for the lack of chewy texture.

	FOODS ALLOWED	**FOODS TO OMIT**
Beverages:	All types—include at least 2 cups of milk daily.	None.
Eggs:	Omelet, scrambled, poached, soft-cooked, or hard-cooked—include at least 1 daily.	Fried eggs.
Fats:	Butter, margarine, light cream, heavy cream, vegetable oils, mayonnaise.	All other salad dressings except mayonnaise.
Cheese:	Cottage cheese, cream cheese, and mild American cheese may be used in cooking.	Strong-flavored sharp cheese.
Breads and cereals:	Enriched white bread, saltines, soda crackers, rusk, zwieback—include 2 to 4 servings daily. Cooked cereals of enriched fine white flour, cornmeal, or strained oatmeal—dry cereals of corn or rice only. Include ½ cup of cereal daily.	Whole-grain bread or rolls, hot breads, pancakes, waffles, whole-grain cereals, all other dry cereals except those on the allowed list.

Vegetables:	Well-cooked asparagus tips, beets, carrots, peas, spinach, string beans, wax beans, tomato juice, winter squash. Include 2 to 3 servings daily, at least 1 green and 1 yellow vegetable.	Broccoli, brussels sprouts, cabbage, cauliflower, celery, lima beans, onions, parsnips, summer squash, tomatoes, turnips, and all raw vegetables.
Fruit:	All canned fruit juices, strained fresh fruit juice, ripe banana. Seedless and skinless, cooked or canned: applesauce, baked apple with skin removed, peeled apricots, light or dark sweet cherries, peaches, and pears. Include 1 serving of citrus juice daily, and 1 to 2 servings of other fruit daily.	All raw fruits except ripe bananas. Cooked or canned: berries, pineapple or other fruits with seeds and skins.
Potato and substitutes:	White or sweet potato without skin — include 1 potato daily. Macaroni, spaghetti, noodles, and rice.	Fried potato, potato chips, roasted potato, potato salad, and whole-grain rice.

Soup: Broth soups, strained cream soups, vegetable soup made with allowed vegetables.

Soups made with dried peas, dried beans, lentils, and onions.

Meat, fish, and poultry: Crisp bacon; baked, broiled, or roasted beef, lamb, veal, chicken, or turkey. Fish: baked, broiled, or creamed fillet of cod, flounder, haddock, sole, halibut, salmon, and swordfish, canned tuna and salmon. Include 6 ounces of meat and/or fish daily. Include calf liver once a week.

Tough fibrous meats with gristle or excess fat. Pork, smoked or salted meats, bologna, corned beef, frankfurters, ham, luncheon meats, sausage, duck, goose, smoked and salted fish. All fried meats, fish, and poultry.

Desserts: Fruit-flavored gelatin with allowed fruits, ice cream, ices, sherbets. Cakes, cookies, and puddings that do not contain nuts, coconut, raisins, seeds, or skins of fruit.

All desserts prepared with nuts, coconut, raisins, seeds, or skins of fruit. All pies, rich pastries.

Miscellaneous: Sugar, jelly, syrup, honey, hard candy, cream sauce, salt, gravy and seasoning in moderation, chocolate, cocoa, vinegar, white sauce, and herbs.

Jams, marmalade, preserves, olives, pickles, popcorn, nuts, garlic, condiments, and all seed spices.

SUGGESTED MENU PLAN

Breakfast
Fruit
Cereal with milk
Egg
Bread with butter
Beverage

Lunch
Meat, fish, or poultry
Potato or substitute
Vegetable
Fruit
Bread with butter
Beverage
Milk

Dinner
Meat, fish, poultry, or eggs
Potato or substitute
Vegetable
Dessert or fruit
Bread with butter
Beverage
Milk

RECIPES

In addition to these recipes for a Soft Diet, the following recipes may also be used:

Beverages:
Double Milk Eggnog 54
Slim Skimnog 54

Eggs:
Baked Eggs in Potatotes 93
Cottage Cheese Omelet 117
Creamed Eggs on Toast 91
Eggs au Gratin 92

Poultry:
Apricot Jellied Turkey Roll 64
Baked Chicken and Apricots 103
Baked Chicken Stew 125
Chicken Stroganoff 123
Chicken Tetrazzini 124
Orange Glazed Chicken 218
Peachy Baked Chicken 217
Peachy Broiled Chicken 103
Poached Breast of Chicken 102
Roast Turkey 64

Fish:
Boiled Fish 104
Broiled Flounder 104
Broiled Flounder Hollandaise 82
Broiled Haddock 65
Halibut Mousse 125
Poached Fish Rolls 65
Poached Haddock 126
Tuna Cheese Casserole 126
Tuna Lasagna 127

Desserts:
Applesauce 104
Baked Lemon Pudding 244
Baked Rice Pudding 107
Banana Gelatin Cup 83
Blancmange (plain) 240
Caramel Pudding 241
Chocolate Cake 128
Coffee Custard 177
Crustless Orange Cheese Pie 128
Cupcakes 248
Gelatin Parfait 106
Poached Pears 105

Rice Cream 106
Snow Pudding 243
Sponge Cake 245
Sugar Cookies 85
Vanilla Pudding 241
Whipped Rice Pudding 107

Soft-Cooked Eggs

2 eggs

Bring water to boil in a small saucepan; reduce heat to a low simmer. Place eggs in water with a slotted spoon. Cook for 4 minutes; remove from water and crack open. Scoop egg out into a small serving dish. Makes 2 servings.

Hard-Cooked Eggs

2 eggs

Place eggs in a small saucepan and cover with water. Bring water to a boil and then reduce heat to a low simmer. Cook for 12 to 15 minutes. Remove from water and rinse immediately under cold water; tap shell gently all over and then peel off. Makes 2 servings.

Scrambled Cottage Cheese

2 eggs
¼ teaspoon salt
1 tablespoon butter
¼ cup cottage cheese

Mix eggs and salt with a fork. Heat butter in a large skillet. Pour in egg mixture. Reduce heat to medium and cook eggs quickly, lifting mixture from bottom and sides of pan as it thickens to allow the thin uncooked part to flow to the bottom. When eggs are almost thickened throughout, stir cottage cheese into egg mixture; the cheese will melt and coat the scrambled eggs. Remove from heat as soon as cheese is melted. Serve at once. Makes 1 or 2 servings.

Cheese Omelet

2 eggs
1 tablespoon water
1 tablespoon butter
¼ cup diced mild American cheese
¼ teaspoon salt

Beat eggs and water together. Melt butter in an 8-inch omelet pan and pour in egg mixture. With a spatula or a fork, carefully draw cooked portions toward the center so that uncooked portion flows to the bottom. Slide pan rapidly back and forth over the heat to keep mixture sliding freely. When partially set, add diced cheese to one side of omelet. Fold other side over cheese and cook several minutes, until omelet is mostly set and cheese is melted. Lift out with a large spatula. Sprinkle with salt. Makes 1 or 2 servings.

Poached Eggs

2 cups water
1 teaspoon vinegar
2 eggs
Salt to taste

Bring water to a boil in a large skillet; add vinegar and reduce heat. Stir a circle in the water and break an egg into the circle; push spreading white back over the yolk with a spoon until it solidifies. Repeat for second egg. Cook for about 4 minutes. Remove eggs with a slotted spoon and serve, sprinkled with salt. Makes 1 or 2 servings.

Baked Egg Florentine

½ cup chopped cooked spinach
1 egg
⅛ teaspoon salt

Preheat oven to 350°F. Butter a small baking dish. Fill with spinach; make a well in the center large enough to hold 1 raw egg. Break egg into depression and sprinkle with salt. Bake 10 to 15 minutes, or until firm. Makes 1 serving.

Blender Mayonnaise

1 egg
½ teaspoon salt
2 tablespoons vinegar
1 cup salad oil

Break egg into electric blender container. Add salt and vinegar and blend. Add ⅓ cup salad oil; blend. Uncover, and blend while pouring the remaining salad oil in a steady stream. Turn off when all oil is absorbed. Makes 1¼ cups mayonnaise. Store in refrigerator in a tightly covered container.

Chicken Broth

1 3½- to 4-pound chicken
2 quarts water
4 carrots, scraped
2 stalks celery with leaves
1 sprig dill
2 teaspoons salt
1 teaspoon sugar

Wash and clean chicken; place in a heavy saucepan with lid. Add water, scraped carrots, celery, dill, salt, and sugar. Bring to a boil, then reduce heat and cover. Simmer for 1½ hours. Strain through fine strainer and discard celery and dill. Reserve carrot to serve as a vegetable or in the soup. Extra broth can be frozen in an ice cube tray and then stored in a plastic bag in the freezer. Chicken can be cut up and served in the soup or served separately. Makes about 2 quarts.

Beef Bouillon

2 pounds beef shin bones
2 pounds lean beef
2 quarts water
1 teaspoon salt
1 bay leaf
1 carrot, scraped
2 stalks celery with leaves

Place bones, beef, and water in a large saucepan. Add salt, bay leaf, carrot, and celery. Bring to a boil and cover; reduce heat and simmer about 3 hours. Skim off fat. Remove bay leaf and celery and discard; reserve carrot to serve in the soup or as a vegetable. Reserve meat to serve separately. Strain remainder of soup and add more salt, if desired. Extra bouillon can be poured into an ice cube tray and frozen, then stored in plastic bags to be used as needed. Makes 2 quarts.

Vegetable Soup

1 quart Chicken Broth (see index)
1 10-ounce package frozen carrots and peas
½ 10-ounce package frozen string beans
2 tablespoons farina cereal
1 teaspoon salt

Pour chicken broth into a large saucepan. Add carrots and peas and string beans. Cover. Heat together until vegetables are well cooked. Add farina and stir through; heat until farina has thickened the soup and is no longer distinguishable. Makes 4 servings.

Dilled Potato Soup

3 potatoes, peeled
1 sprig dill
½ teaspoon salt
3 tablespoons butter
3 tablespoons flour
1 quart milk

Cut potatoes into small pieces and place in a saucepan. Cover with water; add dill and salt. Cook until potatoes are soft, about 20 minutes. Meanwhile, melt butter in a saucepan. Stir in flour until mixture thickens. Stir in milk gradually until smooth and thick. Drain cooked potatoes in a strainer and press through into the milk mixture. Cook and stir until mixture is smooth and thick. Serve at once. Makes 6 servings.

Quick Asparagus Soup

1 cup liquid drained from canned asparagus
1 cup milk
2 tablespoons butter
¼ teaspoon salt

Stir asparagus liquid and milk together in a saucepan. Add butter and salt. Heat. Makes 2 servings.

NOTE: This method can be used with the drained liquid from any vegetable allowed in the diet.

Asparagus with Blender Hollandaise

1 pound fresh asparagus
3 cups water
½ teaspoon salt

Trim asparagus, removing scales and hardened ends. Wash and tie together. Stand asparagus in the bottom of a double boiler. Add water and salt. Cover with the top of the double boiler turned upside down to provide a tall, narrow cooking vessel; this method boils the coarser asparagus bottoms while steaming the tender tips. Cook for 15 to 20 minutes, depending on the thickness of the stalks, until tender. Serve with Blender Hollandaise. Makes 4 servings.

Blender Hollandaise

¼ pound butter
2 egg yolks
2 teaspoons lemon juice
¼ teaspoon salt

Melt butter in a small saucepan. Place egg yolks in an electric blender; add lemon juice and salt. Blend on high and then turn to low and add melted butter a little at a time. Turn blender off at the last drop. Makes 1 cup sauce.

NOTE: This sauce can be refrigerated for several days in a tightly covered jar.

Boiled Beets

1 bunch fresh young beets
Water
½ teaspoon salt

Trim beet tops and root stems, leaving a one-inch top. Wash beets and place in a large saucepan; cover with water and add salt. Cover and cook for about one hour, or until beets are fork-tender. Remove from water and place in a pan of cold water. Rub off the skins and slice, dice, or cut into strips. Add additional salt and butter, if desired. Makes 4 servings.

Harvard Beets #1

2 tablespoons butter
1 tablespoon flour
¼ cup vinegar
¼ cup drained beet juice or water
½ cup sugar
½ teaspoon salt
2 cups boiled beets or canned sliced, drained beets

Melt butter in a saucepan. Add flour and stir until thickened. Add vinegar and beet juice gradually, stirring constantly. Add sugar and salt. Cook until clear, stirring constantly. Add sliced beets and cook to heat through. Makes 4 servings.

Honeyed Carrots

2 cups cooked or canned sliced carrots, drained
2 tablespoons honey
1 tablespoon butter

Drain hot carrots. Add honey and butter and toss lightly until butter is melted and carrots are completely covered with the mixture. Cook over very low heat, stirring constantly, for several minutes. Makes 4 servings.

Baked Acorn Squash

1 medium-sized acorn squash
¼ teaspoon salt
1 tablespoon butter
2 teaspoons soft brown sugar

Preheat oven to 350° F. Cut acorn squash in half and scoop out seeds and stringy membranes. Sprinkle cut sides with salt. Dot centers with butter and sprinkle with soft brown sugar. Place skin side down in a baking dish with a small amount of water. Bake 35 minutes, or until tender. Makes 2 servings.

Easy Creamed Spinach

1 10-ounce package chopped spinach
¼ teaspoon salt
¼ cup dairy sour cream

Cook spinach in a small amount of water with salt added. Drain very well, pressing to remove excess water. Toss with sour cream and serve at once. Makes 2 to 3 servings.

Spinach Soufflé

1 10-ounce package frozen chopped spinach
2 egg whites (use yolks in Blender Hollandaise Sauce; see index)
½ teaspoon salt

Preheat oven to 350° F. Cook and drain spinach well. Beat egg whites until stiff, adding salt during the last stages of beating. Fold spinach through beaten egg whites. Spoon into a buttered baking dish. Bake for 20 minutes, or until firm. Cut into serving portions. Makes 4 servings.

Spinach Cottage Cheese Bake

½ cup cooked chopped spinach
½ cup cottage cheese
¼ teaspoon salt

Preheat oven to 350° F. Spoon spinach into a buttered baking dish. Top with cottage cheese and sprinkle with salt. Bake 15 minutes and serve at once. Makes 1 serving.

Green Beans in Tomato Sauce

1 pound green beans, *or*
  1 10-ounce package frozen cut beans
1 tablespoon butter
1 tablespoon flour
¼ teaspoon salt
1 teaspoon sugar
1 cup tomato juice

Trim fresh beans and cut into 1-inch pieces. Cook in salted water until tender. Melt butter in a saucepan; add flour and cook until thickened. Stir in salt and sugar. Gradually add tomato juice, stirring constantly. When thickened, add drained green beans. Toss and serve at once. Makes 4 servings.

Sweet and Sour Wax Beans

2 cups cooked or canned drained wax beans with liquid
2 tablespoons butter
1 tablespoon flour
2 tablespoons sugar
2 tablespoons lemon juice
¼ teaspoon salt

Cook or heat wax beans. Melt butter in a saucepan; stir in flour and cook until mixture thickens. Stir in sugar, lemon juice, and salt, and gradually stir in 1 cup wax bean liquid. Add hot beans and cook for several minutes. Makes 4 servings.

Baked Sweet Potatoes

2 medium-sized plump sweet potatoes
1 tablespoon butter
¼ cup heavy cream
¼ teaspoon salt

Preheat oven to 350° F. Wash sweet potatoes and bake about 1 hour, or until fork-tender. Remove from oven and scoop out cooked potato, discarding shells. Add butter, cream, and salt to cooked potato and beat well. Makes 2 servings.

Macaroni and Cheese

1 quart water
½ teaspoon salt
1 8-ounce package macaroni
4 slices mild American cheese, diced
1 tablespoon butter

In a deep saucepan, bring salted water to a rolling boil. Add macaroni and cook until very soft, about 10 minutes. Drain. Add diced cheese and butter; toss through hot macaroni until melted. Serve at once. Makes 4 servings.

Orange Rice

1 cup strained orange juice
¾ cup precooked instant rice
1 tablespoon butter
¼ teaspoon salt

Combine orange juice, rice, butter, and salt in a saucepan; bring to a boil. Cover and remove from heat for about 10 minutes. Fluff with a fork every now and then. Makes 2 to 3 servings.

Spaghetti with Creamed Tomato Sauce

1 quart water
½ teaspoon salt
1 8-ounce package spaghetti
2 tablespoons butter
2 tablespoons flour
2 cups tomato juice
½ teaspoon oregano

Bring water and salt to a boil in a large saucepan. Add spaghetti and cook until soft, about 10 to 12 minutes. Meanwhile, melt butter in a small saucepan. Add flour and stir until mixture thickens. Add tomato juice slowly, stirring constantly; add oregano. Cook and stir to a smooth sauce. Drain cooked spaghetti; toss with tomato sauce and serve. Makes 2 to 3 servings.

Fluffy Meat Loaf

1½ pounds ground beef
½ cup tomato juice
1 egg
2 slices white bread
1 small potato
½ teaspoon salt

Preheat oven to 350° F. Place ground beef in a bowl; add tomato juice and egg and work through meat. Soak white bread with water and tear into bits; add to meat and work through. Peel and grate potato into meat; add salt and mix well. Pack into a loaf pan and bake 1¼ to 1½ hours, depending on rareness desired. Makes 6 servings.

Baked Beef Stew

2 pounds beef, chunked
2 cups tomato juice
1 bay leaf
3 potatoes, peeled and quartered
3 carrots, scraped and chunked
1 teaspoon salt

Preheat oven to 350° F. Place beef in a small Dutch oven or similar baking pot with tight lid. Add tomato juice, bay leaf, potatoes, and carrots. Sprinkle with salt. Cover tightly and bake 1½ hours, adding additional water or tomato juice if needed. Makes 6 servings.

Chicken in the Pot

1 3½- to 4-pound chicken, cleaned
2 cups chicken broth
2 sprigs dill
½ teaspoon salt
3 carrots, scraped and cut into chunks
1 10-ounce package frozen peas
Cooked noodles

Preheat oven to 350° F. Place chicken in a small Dutch oven or similar baking pot with tight lid. Add chicken broth, dill, salt, and carrots. Cover and bake 1½ hours. After 45 minutes, add frozen peas. Finish baking and serve on bed of cooked noodles. Makes 4 servings.

Baked Orange Chicken

1 3½- to 4-pound chicken, cut up
1 cup orange juice, strained
½ teaspoon salt

Preheat oven to 350°F. Arrange chicken in a baking pan and pour orange juice over pieces. Sprinkle with salt. Bake for 1 hour. Makes 4 servings.

Broiled Lemon Flounder

2 pieces fillet of flounder
½ cup strained lemon juice
¼ teaspoon salt

Arrange fillets in a small baking dish about 2 hours before cooking and pour lemon juice over both pieces. Refrigerate until cooking time. Then sprinkle with salt and place in a preheated broiler for 5 to 7 minutes, or until fish flakes easily. Lemon juice will evaporate and fish will be very tender. Makes 2 servings.

Baked Apple

2 large apples
2 tablespoons butter
1 tablespoon soft brown sugar

Preheat oven to 350° F. Wash and core apples, leaving the bottom end intact. Remove about 1 inch of peel from the top. Put half the butter and brown sugar into each apple cavity. Place apples in a small baking dish and pour in about 1 inch water. Bake for 30 minutes, or until apple is tender but retains its shape. Serve with heavy cream, if desired. Makes 2 servings.

NOTE: The skin of the apple should not be eaten, or it should be carefully removed before serving.

Banana Freeze

1 ripe banana
2 tablespoons strained lemon juice
1 cup heavy cream
¼ cup confectioners' sugar

Cut up banana and place in an electric blender with the lemon juice; blend until pureed. Whip cream with an electric or hand beater; as it thickens add sugar. Fold pureed bananas through whipped cream. Spoon into an ice cube tray and freeze. Makes 2 to 3 servings.

Banana-Lime Gelatin

1 3-ounce package lime gelatin
1 cup boiling water
1 cup cold water
1 sliced ripe banana
½ cup well-cooked peas (optional)

Add boiling water to gelatin and stir until all crystals are dissolved; add cold water and stir well. Add banana and cooked peas. Spoon into individual serving dishes or into a 3-cup mold. Chill for several hours, until firm. Makes 4 servings.

Peachy Gelatin

1 3-ounce package orange gelatin
1 8-ounce can sliced peaches, with juice
1 cup boiling water

Empty gelatin into a bowl. Drain sliced peaches into a measuring cup; add enough water to make 1 cup liquid. Pour boiling water into gelatin and stir to dissolve; add peach/water liquid and sliced peaches. Spoon into individual serving dishes or into a 3-cup mold. Chill for several hours, until firm. Makes 4 servings.

Creamy Rice Pudding

1 cup uncooked white rice
1 cup water
½ teaspoon salt
2½ cups milk
½ cup honey
1 tablespoon butter
½ pint heavy cream, whipped

Combine rice, water, and salt in the top of a double boiler. Bring to boil and cook 5 minutes. Add milk and return to a boil; place over boiling water, cover and continue cooking for about 25 minutes, or until liquid is absorbed. Remove from heat and stir in honey and butter. Chill. Fold in 1 cup whipped cream; spoon into dessert dishes and top with remaining whipped cream. Makes 8 servings.

Chocolate Chiffon Pudding

1 envelope (1 tablespoon) unflavored gelatin
¼ cup unsweetened cocoa
4 tablespoons sugar
⅛ teaspoon salt
2 eggs, separated
2 cups milk
1½ teaspoons vanilla

In a saucepan, mix together gelatin, cocoa, 2 tablespoons sugar, and salt. Beat together egg yolks and milk; stir into gelatin mixture. Place over very low heat, stirring constantly, until gelatin dissolves and mixture thickens slightly. Remove from heat and stir in vanilla. Chill, stirring occasionally, until mixture is thick but not lumpy. Beat egg whites until soft peaks form; gradually add remaining 2 tablespoons of sugar and beat stiff. Fold gelatin mixture into beaten egg whites. Turn into a 1-quart mold or spoon into individual serving dishes. Makes 6 servings.

Crustless Cream Cheese Pie

1 pound cream cheese
2 eggs
¾ cup sugar
1 teaspoon vanilla
2 teaspoons lemon juice

Preheat oven to 375°F. Mash cream cheese until creamy; add eggs and beat well. Add sugar, then vanilla and lemon juice. Beat well, until smooth. Pour into a buttered 9-inch pie pan and bake about 25 minutes, until firm. Turn off oven and let pie come to room temperature in oven; remove after an hour or so. Chill. Makes 8 servings.

Vanilla Cookies

1 cup butter
½ cup sugar
1 egg
2½ cups flour
1 teaspoon vanilla

Preheat oven to 425°F. Cream butter and sugar well. Add egg, mixing well; add flour and vanilla. Pack into a cookie press and press onto a greased cookie sheet. If no cookie press is available, shape dough into a long log by rolling in waxed paper; then slice into ¼-inch discs. Bake about 8 minutes, or until edges are lightly browned. Makes about 3 dozen cookies.

5

The Strict Bland Diet

The strict bland diet is most often prescribed for ulcer patients leaving the hospital for home. Just keep in mind that many small meals are better than a few large ones, so it's better to divide the menu into six or more small meals a day. No meat, except tender chicken, turkey, and fish, is allowed. Fruit juices should be served during a meal rather than between meals, so your doctor will probably order milk drinks between meals. The new thinking is that skim milk will do; this is a point to discuss with the person who prescribes the diet.

Careful menu planning allows well-balanced nutrition for you or your patient. Pay particular attention to the color scheme of the food; otherwise this diet can get boring. It's a perfect time to use brightly colored pottery and china accessories to pep up your meals.

	FOODS ALLOWED	**FOODS TO OMIT**
Beverages:	Milk and milk drinks.	All others.
Eggs:	Omelet; scrambled, poached, soft-cooked, or hard-cooked—include at least 1 daily.	Fried eggs.
Fats:	Butter, margarine, cream cheese.	All others.
Cheese:	Cottage cheese, cream cheese, mild American cheese.	All others.
Breads and cereals:	White toast or white crackers; cooked farina, cream of wheat, cream of rice, strained oatmeal.	Fresh bread, whole-grain breads, crackers, rolls, and quick breads, except those permitted. All cereals, including all dry cereals and whole-grain cereals, except those permitted.
Vegetables:	Pureed: asparagus, beets, carrots, peas, spinach, winter squash, string beans, wax beans.	All others.
Fruit:	Strained fruit juices. Pureed applesauce, peaches, pears, and apricots.	All others.

Potato and substitutes:	White potatoes, mashed, creamed, scalloped, and baked (do not serve skin). Rice, plain noodles, macaroni, and spaghetti.	All others.
Soup:	Strained homemade cream soups, made with allowed vegetables and white potatoes.	All broths, meat stock, cream soups made with meat stock, and all commercial soups.
Meat, fish, and poultry:	Minced or tender sliced chicken and turkey. White fish fillets.	All others.
Desserts:	Fruit-flavored gelatin, rennet custards, soft custards, vanilla ice cream, vanilla or butterscotch puddings (all without chocolate, coconut, fruit, or nuts). Angel food cake.	All others.
Miscellaneous:	Salt, white sauce, mild herbs. Creamy peanut butter, sugar, jelly, syrup, honey, hard candy, chocolate, and cocoa.	Pepper; all other spices, condiments; coconut, nuts, olives, pickles, relishes, vinegar; meat extracts and meat gravy. All other candy.

SUGGESTED MENU PLAN

Breakfast
Fruit or juice
Cereal
Egg
White toast
Butter
Milk

Mid-morning
Milk and
crackers

Lunch
Cream soup
Cheese or egg dish
Pureed vegetable
White toast
Butter
Fruit
Milk

Mid-afternoon
Dessert
Milk

Dinner
Cream soup
Chicken or fish
Potato
Pureed vegetable
White toast
Butter
Dessert
Milk

Bedtime
Milk
White toast
Butter

RECIPES

In addition to these recipes for a strict bland diet, the following recipes may also be used:

Beverages:

Eggs:

Vegetables:

Potato and substitutes:

Poultry:

Fish:

Desserts:

Double Milk Eggnog

1¾ cups dry powdered low-fat milk
1½ tablespoons sugar
3¼ cups whole milk
1 teaspoon vanilla
1 egg

Combine all ingredients in a large mixing bowl. Beat with electric mixer or hand beater until mixture is frothy. Refrigerate. Makes 1 quart.

Slim Skimnog

2 cups dry powdered low-fat milk
1½ tablespoons sugar
3¼ cups skim milk
1 teaspoon vanilla
1 egg white

Combine nonfat dry milk, sugar, skim milk, vanilla, and egg white in a large bowl; mix with electric or hand beater until frothy. Refrigerate. Makes 1 quart.

Peanut Butter Omelet

2 eggs
1 tablespoon cold water
1 tablespoon butter
2 tablespoons creamy peanut butter

Beat together eggs and water with a fork. Melt butter in a small skillet and pour in egg. Mixture should immediately set at edges. With a spatula or a fork, carefully draw cooked portions toward center, so that uncooked portion flows to the bottom. Slide pan rapidly back and forth over heat to keep mixture sliding freely. When mixture is partially set, dot top with creamy peanut butter and stir into egg. When set, remove from heat, fold over, and roll out onto plate. Serve at once. Makes 1 or 2 servings.

Carrot Soufflé

3 tablespoons butter
3 tablespoons flour
1 cup hot milk
3 eggs, separated
¼ teaspoon salt
1 cup cooked pureed carrots

Preheat oven to 350° F. Melt butter in a saucepan; add flour and stir until it is thick and bubbly. Stir in milk gradually. Beat together egg yolks and salt; stir in milk mixture and then pureed carrots. Beat egg whites until stiff peaks form; fold into carrot mixture. Spoon into a well-buttered 1-quart ring mold. Set mold into a pan with 1 inch of hot water covering bottom and bake for 35 minutes, until firm. Loosen edges and turn out onto platter. Makes 6 servings.

NOTE: Substitutions can be made with any allowed vegetable.

Strained Cream Soup #1

2 cups half-and-half cream
1 cup cooked allowed vegetables
½ cup liquid from cooked vegetables
¼ teaspoon salt

Pour cream into a saucepan. Combine cooked vegetables, liquid, and salt in an electric blender; blend on high to puree. Pour through strainer into cream. Heat and stir until smooth. Makes 6 servings.

Strained Cream Soup #2

1 cup cooked vegetables
½ cup liquid from cooked vegetables
2 tablespoons butter
2 tablespoons flour
1 cup milk
¼ teaspoon salt

Combine cooked vegetables and liquid in an electric blender, blending on high to puree. Set aside. In a saucepan, melt butter; stir in flour and cook until thick, stirring constantly. Gradually stir in milk, and add salt. Pour vegetables through a strainer into the milk mixture. Heat and stir until smooth. Makes 4 servings.

Pureed Asparagus Tips

½ pound fresh asparagus, *or*
   1 16-ounce can asparagus
¼ teaspoon dried tarragon, marjoram, or thyme
½ teaspoon salt
1 teaspoon butter
1 teaspoon strained lemon juice

Trim fresh asparagus to remove scales and hard ends and tie in a bunch. Stand asparagus in the bottom of a double boiler. Fill pan with water, add tarragon and salt, and cover with the top of the double boiler turned upside down to create a tall pot. Cook for 20 minutes, or until tender. If using canned asparagus, heat with tarragon or other herb. Drain, reserving liquid. Cut off three to four inches of the tips, reserving rest of asparagus for another dinner. Place tips in an electric blender. Add ¼ cup reserved cooking liquid and blend until asparagus is completely pureed. Add butter and lemon juice and blend again, adding more cooking liquid if needed to get the right consistency. Makes 2 servings.

NOTE: Remaining reserved canned liquid can be used to flavor cream soup. Remaining reserved fresh asparagus liquid can be boiled further to reduce the volume and then used in the same way. For additional ways to puree vegetables, refer to Pureed Vegetables for Creamed Soup (see index).

Pureed Carrots

4 fresh carrots, *or*
   1 16-ounce can sliced carrots
¼ teaspoon dried dill, rosemary, or thyme
½ teaspoon salt
1 teaspoon butter

Trim and scrape carrots and cut in slices. Place in a saucepan, cover with water, and add dried dill and salt. Cook for 15 to 20 minutes, or until very tender. If using canned carrots, heat with dill or other herbs. Drain, reserving liquid. Place carrots in an electric blender with ¼ cup reserved liquid; blend until carrots are completely pureed. Add butter and blend again, adding more cooking liquid if needed to get the right consistency. Makes 2 servings.

NOTE: Remaining reserved canned liquid can be used to flavor cream soup. Remaining reserved fresh carrot liquid can be boiled further to reduce the volume and then used in the same way. For additional ways to puree vegetables, refer to Pureed Vegetables for Creamed Soup (see index).

Pureed Peas

1 pound fresh peas, *or*
  1 10-ounce package frozen peas, *or*
  1 16-ounce can peas
¼ teaspoon dried marjoram or rosemary
½ teaspoon salt
1 teaspoon butter

Shell fresh peas. Place fresh or frozen peas in a saucepan and cover with water; add dried marjoram and salt. Cook 15 to 20 minutes, or until very tender. If using canned peas, add marjoram and heat. Drain. Force peas through a strainer or a food mill. Stir in butter. Makes 4 servings.

NOTE: Leftover pureed vegetables can be refrigerated in tightly closed containers for 2 days. Remaining liquid can be used to flavor cream soup, after boiling to reduce volume. For additional ways to puree vegetables, refer to Pureed Vegetables for Creamed Soup (see index).

Pureed Spinach

1 pound fresh spinach, *or*
  1 16-ounce package frozen chopped spinach
¼ teaspoon oregano, rosemary, or thyme
½ teaspoon salt
1 teaspoon butter

Wash and trim fresh spinach. Place fresh or frozen spinach in a saucepan and cover with water; add oregano and salt. Cook 15 to 20 minutes, or until very tender. Drain, reserving liquid. Place spinach in an electric blender with ¼ cup reserved liquid; blend until completely pureed. Add butter and blend again, adding more cooking liquid if needed to get the right consistency. Makes 4 servings.

NOTE: Leftover pureed vegetables can be refrigerated in tightly closed containers for 2 days. Remaining reserved liquids can be boiled further to reduce the volume and then used to flavor cream soup. For additional methods of pureeing vegetables, refer to Pureed Vegetables for Creamed Soup (see index).

Pureed String Beans

1 pound fresh string beans, *or*
  1 10-ounce package frozen beans, *or*
  1 16-ounce can beans
¼ teaspoon dried basil, oregano, or thyme
½ teaspoon salt
1 teaspoon butter

Wash and trim fresh string beans. Place fresh or frozen beans in a saucepan, cover with water, and add basil and salt. Cook 15 to 20 minutes, until very tender. If using canned beans, add basil and heat. Drain, reserving liquid. Place string beans in an electric blender with ¼ cup reserved liquid; blend until beans are completely pureed. Add butter and blend again, adding more cooking liquid if needed to get the right consistency. Makes 4 servings.

NOTE: Leftover pureed vegetables can be refrigerated in tightly closed containers for 2 days. Remaining reserved liquid can be boiled further to reduce the volume and then used to flavor cream soup. Remaining canned liquid can be used as is. For additional ways to puree vegetables, refer to Pureed Vegetables for Creamed Soup (see index).

Pureed Wax Beans

1 **pound fresh wax beans,** *or*
  1 **10-ounce package frozen beans,** *or*
  1 **16-ounce can beans**
¼ **teaspoon dried dill or mint**
½ **teaspoon salt**
1 **teaspoon butter**

Wash and trim fresh wax beans. Place fresh or frozen beans in a saucepan, cover with water, and add dill and salt. Cook 15 to 20 minutes, until very tender. If using canned beans, add dill and heat. Drain, reserving liquid. Place wax beans in an electric blender with ¼ cup reserved liquid and blend until beans are completely pureed. Add butter and blend again, adding more cooking liquid if needed to get the right consistency. Makes 4 servings.

NOTE: Leftover pureed vegetables can be refrigerated in tightly closed containers for 2 days. Remaining reserved liquid can be boiled further to reduce the volume and then used to flavor cream soup. Remaining canned liquid can be used as is. For additional ways to puree vegetables, refer to Pureed Vegetables for Creamed Soup (see index).

Pureed Acorn Squash

1 acorn squash
2 teaspoons butter
2 teaspoons soft brown sugar
¼ teaspoon salt
¼ cup milk or cream

Preheat oven to 350° F. Cut squash in half and remove the seeds and membranes. Place in a baking dish and pour in about 1 inch of water. Dot squash cavities with butter and sprinkle with sugar; sprinkle rims with salt. Bake for 45 minutes, until very soft. Remove squash and scoop out of shells; mash well with milk or cream, or place in electric blender and puree. Makes 4 servings.

NOTE: Leftover squash can be refrigerated in a tightly closed container for 2 days. For additional methods of pureeing vegetables, refer to Pureed Vegetables for Creamed Soup (see index).

Cheesy Mashed Potatoes

6 medium potatoes
3 tablespoons butter
⅓ cup hot milk
½ teaspoon salt
2 slices mild American cheese, diced

Scrub, pare, and quarter potatoes; place in a large saucepan and cover with water. Cook 20 to 30 minutes, until fork-tender. Drain. Add butter, hot milk, and salt. Mash well, using hand electric mixer if desired. Add cheese and mix until cheese is melted. Makes 6 servings.

Scalloped Potatoes

4 large raw potatoes
2 tablespoons butter
2 tablespoons flour
1 cup milk
¼ teaspoon salt

Preheat oven to 350° F. Peel and slice potatoes ½ inch thick; set aside in a bowl of cold water. Melt butter in a saucepan; add flour and stir constantly until bubbly. Gradually stir in milk and continue stirring until mixture thickens. Add salt and remove from heat. Drain potatoes. Place a layer of overlapping potato slices on the bottom of a greased baking dish; cover with a thin layer of white sauce. Repeat with layers of potatoes and sauce, finishing with sauce. Bake 1 hour, or until potatoes are soft. Makes 4 servings.

Noodles and Cottage Cheese

1 quart water
½ teaspoon salt
1 8-ounce package broad noodles
1 teaspoon sugar
½ cup cottage cheese
2 tablespoons butter

Preheat oven to 350°F. Bring water and salt to a rolling boil. Add noodles and cook for 10 minutes, or until soft. Drain. Mix noodles with sugar and cottage cheese, spoon into a buttered casserole, and dot the top with butter. Bake 15 minutes. Makes 4 servings.

Apricot Jellied Turkey Roll

1 4- to 6-pound turkey roll, thawed
1 small jar pureed apricots (baby food)
2 tablespoons currant jelly
1 tablespoon butter

Preheat oven to 350° F. Arrange turkey roll in a roasting pan. In a small saucepan, combine pureed apricots, jelly, and butter. Heat and stir until jelly and butter are melted. Spoon mixture over turkey roll, covering the surface as much as possible. Bake 2 to 2½ hours; slice and serve. Makes 6 to 8 servings.

Roast Turkey

1 turkey
½ teaspoon salt
½ cup melted butter

Preheat oven to 350° F. Clean and rinse turkey and pat dry; rub salt on interior and exterior surfaces. Place in a large roasting pan and paint entire skin surface with melted butter, reserving some for later basting. Cover top of turkey loosely with a large piece of aluminum foil. Roast about 20 minutes to the pound, or until turkey leg moves easily when jiggled. Baste several times with remaining melted butter; remove foil during last hour to brown turkey. Remove from oven and let turkey "rest" for 20 minutes before carving.

NOTE: When turkey is removed from roasting pan, pour boiling water into pan to make several cups of gravy. When freezing turkey slices, cover with gravy to retain moisture.

Broiled Haddock

1½ pounds haddock fillets
2 tablespoons butter
½ teaspoon salt
3 tablespoons lemon juice, strained

Arrange fillets on broiling pan and dot with tiny pieces of butter; sprinkle with salt and lemon juice. Broil 10 minutes in preheated broiler, or until fish flakes easily. Makes 4 servings.

Poached Fish Rolls

4 fillets of sole
1 3½-ounce package cream cheese
2 tablespoons milk
1 cup cream
1 sprig fresh dill, cut fine, with stems removed
¼ teaspoon salt

Spread fillets with cream cheese mixed with milk. Roll up fillets and place in a small skillet. Pour cream over rolls and sprinkle with dill and salt; cover tightly and cook over low heat for 15 to 20 minutes, or until fish flakes easily. Makes 4 servings.

Angel Food Cake

12 egg whites
¼ teaspoon salt
1 teaspoon cream of tartar
1¼ cups granulated sugar
1 cup confectioners' sugar
1¼ cups cake flour
1 tablespoon lemon juice

Preheat oven to 350° F. Let egg whites come to room temperature for greatest volume; add salt and beat until foamy. Add cream of tartar and beat until soft peaks form. Sift together sugars and cake flour; fold into egg whites. Fold in lemon juice. Pour into an ungreased 10-inch tube pan and bake for 50 to 60 minutes. Remove from oven and invert tube onto neck of an empty soda bottle, hanging cake upside down to cool. This will prevent it from collapsing. Makes 1 ten-inch cake.

NOTE: Extra yolks can be used to make Blender Hollandaise or, substituting 2 yolks for each whole egg called for, Blender Mayonnaise (see index).

6

The Regular Bland Diet

This diet is prescribed for many troubles along the digestive tract because it's nonirritating and easy to digest. Ulcer patients may need smaller portions and between-meal snacks and milk.

Food should be warm rather than very hot or very cold. All pits, skins, and seeds should be removed, and food should be eaten slowly and chewed well. Fruit juices should be served with the meal and taken after some of the food has been eaten.

A large variety of foods is allowed, so patients can have a nutritionally adequate and nonboring diet. Plan menus to take advantage of the variety of foods that is allowed on this diet, and bear in mind that colorful presentation plays an important role in keeping your appetite and your spirits up.

	FOODS ALLOWED	FOODS TO OMIT
Beverages:	Milk and milk drinks—include at least 2 cups daily. Decaffeinated coffee, weak tea.	Coffee, strong tea, cocoa, chocolate milk, all carbonated beverages, all alcoholic beverages.
Eggs:	Omelet; scrambled, poached, soft-cooked, or hard-cooked—include at least 1 daily.	Fried eggs
Fats:	Butter, light cream, heavy cream, salad oil.	All others.
Cheese:	Cream cheese, cottage cheese, mild American cheese.	All others.
Breads and cereals:	White or rye bread without seeds, either one day old or toasted. White melba toast, saltines, soda crackers, zwieback, matzoh. Cooked enriched fine white cereals and well-cooked strained oatmeal. Dry cereals: only corn and rice flakes and puffed rice. Include 2 to 4 slices of bread daily, and 1 serving of cereal.	Rye bread with seeds, pumpernickel bread, hot breads, biscuits, any rolls or breads with seeds, whole-grain bread and crackers, bran, coarse cereals, whole-grain cereals. All others except those allowed.

Vegetables:	Cooked asparagus tips, carrots, beets, peas, spinach, swiss chard, string beans, wax beans, winter squash, tomato juice —include 3 to 4 servings daily, including 1 green and 1 yellow.	All others.
Fruit:	Strained fruit juices, ripe banana. Applesauce, peeled apricots, peaches, pears (no seeds or skins), canned Royal Anne cherries—include 1 to 2 servings of fruit and 1 serving of citrus juice daily.	All others, including all raw fruit except ripe banana, cooked or canned berries, pineapple, and fruit with skins or seeds, even if cooked.
Potato and substitutes:	Boiled, baked (do not serve skin), mashed white or sweet potato. Barley, macaroni, noodles, spaghetti, white rice. Include 1 potato daily.	Fried potato, roasted potato, potato chips, whole-grain rice.
Soup:	Cream soups made from allowed vegetables.	All broths and meat stock soups, cream soups made with meat stock, all commercial soups.

Meat, fish, and poultry:	Beef, veal, lamb, pork, calf liver, white-flesh fish, canned tuna and salmon, oysters, chicken, turkey, and sweetbreads. All meat must be tender and free of coarse connective fibers. Include 2 servings daily, and liver once a week.	Duck, goose, fried meats; lobster, crabmeat, shrimp; smoked and spiced meats and fish, all other fish.
Desserts:	Sponge cake, angel food cake, plain sugar wafers, vanilla wafers, custard, fruit-flavored gelatin, vanilla ice cream, plain ices, plain sherbet, rennet custards, plain puddings (except chocolate-flavored).	All desserts prepared with chocolate, coconut, nuts, or raisins. No seeds, skins, spices, whole fruits, pies, pastries, or rich cakes.
Miscellaneous:	Salt, vanilla, cinnamon, paprika, vegetable oils; oregano, basil, rosemary, marjoram, thyme, tarragon, lemon juice, vinegar; creamy peanut butter; sugar, jelly, syrup, honey, hard candy.	Condiments, salad dressings, gravy; cloves, garlic, ginger, mace, mint, fresh parsley, pepper, pickles; popcorn, nuts; spices with seeds; jam, preserves, marmalade, molasses, all candy other than hard candy.

SUGGESTED MENU PLAN

Breakfast
Fruit juice
Cereal with milk
Egg
Bread with butter
Milk
Hot beverage

Mid-morning
Milk and crackers

Lunch
Meat, fish, or poultry
Vegetable
Potato or substitute
Fruit
Bread with butter
Milk

Mid-afternoon
Milk
Dessert

Dinner
Cream soup
Meat, fish, poultry, or egg
Vegetable
Potato or substitute
Dessert or fruit
Bread with butter
Milk

Bedtime
Milk
Toast and butter

RECIPES

In addition to these recipes for a regular bland diet, the following recipes may also be used:

Beverages:
Eggnog 19
Double Milk Eggnog 54
Orange Eggnog 19
Slim Skimnog 54

Eggs:
Baked Egg Florentine 32
Carrot Soufflé 55
Cheese Omelet 31
Grape Soufflé 74
Hard-Cooked Eggs 30
Poached Eggs 31
Soft-Cooked Eggs 30
Spinach Soufflé 38

Vegetables:
Asparagus with Blender Hollandaise 35
Baked Acorn Squash 37
Boiled Beets 36
Creamy Pureed Squash 97
Easy Creamed Spinach 38
Green Beans in Tomato Sauce 39
Harvard Beets 37 230
Honeyed Carrots 37
Spinach Cottage Cheese Bake 38
Sweet and Sour Wax Beans 39

Potatoes and substitutes:
  Baked Sweet Potatoes 40
  Cheesy Mashed Potatoes 62
  Creamy Mashed Potatoes 97
  Noodles and Cottage Cheese 63
  Noodle Peach Bake 98
  Macaroni and Cheese 40
  Orange Rice 40
  Scalloped Potatoes 63
  Spaghetti with Creamed Tomato Sauce 41

Fruit:
  Baked Apple 44

Soup:
  Creamed Soup for Pureed Vegetables 21
  Pureed Vegetables for Creamed Soup 20
  Strained Cream Soup #1 56
  Strained Cream Soup #2 56

Meat:
  Baked Beef Stew 42
  Fluffy Meat Loaf 41

Poultry:
  Apricot Jellied Turkey Roll 64
  Baked Chicken and Apricots 103
  Baked Orange Chicken 43
  Chicken in the Pot 42
  Roast Turkey 64

Fish:
  Broiled Flounder 104
  Broiled Haddock 65
  Broiled Lemon Flounder 43
  Poached Fish Rolls 65

Desserts:

Grape Soufflé

¾ cup grape jelly

2 teaspoons lemon juice

3 egg whites, at room temperature

⅛ teaspoon cream of tartar

⅛ teaspoon salt

3 tablespoons sugar

Preheat oven to 350° F. Heat jelly in a saucepan until melted; add lemon juice. Beat egg whites with salt and cream of tartar until soft peaks form; then beat in sugar a little at a time until stiff. Fold about 2 cups of beaten whites into jelly; then fold in remaining whites. Pour into a 6-cup soufflé dish and bake for 20 to 25 minutes. Makes 6 servings.

Carrot Strips

6 carrots, cut in lengthwise strips

½ cup water

2 tablespoons butter

1 tablespoon sugar

½ teaspoon salt

Place carrot strips in a heavy saucepan. Add water, butter, sugar, and salt. Cover and simmer 20 minutes, or until carrots are tender, adding a little more water if necessary. Makes 4 to 6 servings.

Squash Rings

1 acorn squash
½ teaspoon salt
½ teaspoon sugar
1 tablespoon butter

Peel acorn squash and cut crosswise into thick rings. Remove all seeds and membranes. Place squash rings in a large skillet, sprinkle with salt and sugar, and dot with butter. Add about ½ inch water to the skillet. Cover and simmer 20 to 25 minutes, until squash is fork-tender. Remove with a spatula. Makes 4 servings.

Spinach in Orange-Butter Sauce

1 10-ounce package frozen whole-leaf spinach
¼ teaspoon salt
¼ cup strained orange juice
2 tablespoons butter

Cook spinach with salt and a small amount of water, until tender. Drain. Combine orange juice and butter in a small saucepan; heat and stir until butter is melted. Pour sauce over spinach and toss. Makes 3 to 4 servings.

Tender Peas

1½ pounds fresh peas, shelled, *or*
   1 10-ounce package frozen peas
2 cups water
½ teaspoon salt
1 teaspoon sugar
¼ teaspoon rosemary
1 tablespoon butter

Place peas in a saucepan. Add water, salt, sugar, and rosemary. Bring to a boil, then lower heat and simmer for 15 minutes, until peas are very tender. Drain; toss with butter and serve. Makes 4 servings.

Baked Stuffed Potatoes

2 large baking potatoes
2 tablespoons butter
2 tablespoons mild American cheese
¼ teaspoon salt

Preheat oven to 350° F. Wash and dry potatoes; bake for 1 hour or until fork-tender. Remove from oven and cut in half lengthwise; scoop potato out of shells, reserving shells for filling. Mash potatoes with butter, cheese, and salt. Refill shells and return to oven for 5 minutes. Makes 4 servings.

NOTE: These stuffed potatoes can be frozen for later use—reheat frozen stuffed potatoes at 350° F. for 20 to 25 minutes. Do not eat the potato skin.

Boiled Barley

½ cup barley
1 quart boiling water
1 teaspoon salt
1 teaspoon butter

Place barley in a saucepan; pour boiling water over it and stir. Add salt. Bring to a boil and cook for 1 hour, adding more boiling water if necessary. Toss with butter when done. Makes 4 servings.

Cheesy Rice

2 tablespoons butter
2 tablespoons flour
1 cup milk
½ teaspoon salt
1 cup shredded mild American cheese
3 cups cooked rice

Preheat oven to 350° F. Melt butter, stir in flour, and mix until bubbly. Gradually stir in milk until smooth. Add salt and half the cheese and stir until cheese is melted and sauce is thick. Place cooked rice in a buttered 1-quart baking dish. Pour sauce over rice and top with remaining cheese. Cover and bake for 30 minutes; uncover and bake 5 minutes longer. Makes 6 servings.

Herb Rice

1 cup uncooked rice
2 cups water
½ teaspoon salt
½ teaspoon rosemary
2 tablespoons butter

Combine rice, water, salt, rosemary, and butter; heat to boiling and stir. Cover and simmer for 14 minutes, or until tender. Makes 6 half-cup servings.

Rice-Stuffed Peaches

4 large canned peach halves (skinless)
½ cup cooked rice
1 teaspoon sugar
⅛ teaspoon cinnamon
1 tablespoon butter

Drain peach halves and place rounded side down in a flat baking dish. Combine rice, sugar, and cinnamon; spoon into cavities in peach halves. Dot with butter. Place in preheated broiler for 5 minutes. Makes 4 servings.

Broiled Bananas

2 bananas
1 tablespoon lemon juice, strained
1½ tablespoons honey

Peel bananas and cut in half lengthwise; if very long, cut in half crosswise. Sprinkle with lemon juice and arrange in a buttered baking pan with rounded sides up; brush with honey. Place in preheated broiler for 5 minutes, or until lightly browned. Makes 4 servings.

Veal Stew

1 pound veal, cut into bite-sized chunks
2 potatoes, peeled and quartered
4 carrots, peeled and chunked
½ pound fresh string beans, trimmed
1½ cups tomato juice
½ teaspoon rosemary
½ teaspoon salt

Preheat oven to 350° F. Place veal in a small Dutch oven or other heavy container with tight lid. Add potatoes, carrots, and string beans, then tomato juice, rosemary, and salt. Cover and bake 2 hours, or until meat is fork-tender. Makes 4 servings.

Broiled Calf Liver

1 pound calf liver, cut in ¼-inch slices
½ teaspoon salt
2 tablespoons flour
2 tablespoons butter or margarine, melted

Wash liver, and pat dry. Sprinkle with salt. Dust with flour, shaking off excess, and place liver slices in a broiling pan. Set in preheated broiler for 2 to 3 minutes on each side; remove to platter and pour melted butter over slices. Makes 4 servings.

Baked Breaded Sweetbreads

1 pound sweetbreads
2 cups boiling water
½ teaspoon salt
1 tablespoon lemon juice
¼ cup melted butter
¼ cup finely ground toasted white bread crumbs

Soak sweetbreads in cold water for about 20 minutes; cook in boiling water, with salt and lemon juice, for 10 minutes. Preheat oven to 350° F. Remove all skin, pipes, and membranes. Dip into melted butter and then into crumbs. Bake in a buttered baking dish for 30 minutes, basting occasionally with remaining melted butter. Makes 4 servings.

Baked Chicken with Peaches

1 broiler chicken, cut in serving pieces
1 tablespoon flour
½ teaspoon salt
2 tablespoons butter
1 1-pound can peach halves, with syrup
½ teaspoon cinnamon

Preheat oven to 350° F. Place chicken pieces in a flat baking dish. Combine flour and salt and sprinkle over chicken; dot with butter. Bake for 30 minutes. Place peach halves around chicken; spoon some of the syrup over chicken and peaches. Sprinkle with cinnamon. Return to oven for an additional 20 to 30 minutes. Makes 4 servings.

Broiled Tarragon Chicken

1 broiler chicken, quartered
½ teaspoon salt
¼ cup salad oil
⅓ cup lemon juice (strained)
1 teaspoon dried tarragon

Arrange chicken in a flat baking dish. Sprinkle with salt. Combine salad oil, lemon juice, and tarragon; pour over chicken and let marinate for an hour in the refrigerator before broiling. Turn occasionally. Place in preheated broiler for 30 minutes; turn and broil 15 minutes longer, or until fork-tender. Makes 4 servings.

Chicken Livers Oregano

1 pound chicken livers
1½ cups water
½ teaspoon salt
¼ teaspoon oregano

Wash and trim chicken livers. Place in a skillet with water, salt, and oregano and simmer 10 minutes, turning occasionally. Remove with a slotted spoon and serve on toasted white bread. Makes 4 servings.

Chopped Liver and Bean Spread

1 pound chicken livers
1½ cups water
½ teaspoon salt
¼ teaspoon rosemary
1 hard-cooked egg
½ cup canned French-style cut green beans
¼ teaspoon salt

Wash and trim chicken livers. Place in a skillet with water, salt, and rosemary and simmer 10 minutes, turning occasionally. Remove from water with a slotted spoon; reserve liquid. With a meat grinder, grind livers, egg, and green beans together. Add salt. If mixture is too dry, carefully add liquid in which livers were cooked, using only as many teaspoonfuls as the mixture readily absorbs. Chill and serve with crackers. Makes 1½ to 2 cups of spread.

Broiled Flounder Hollandaise

2 slices fillet of flounder
¼ cup Blender Hollandaise Sauce (see index)
1 ripe banana
Dash paprika

Wash and dry fillets and arrange on a broiling pan. Spread half the Hollandaise Sauce thinly over fillets. Peel banana and slice lengthwise in half; place pieces cut side down on fillets. Top with remaining sauce and sprinkle with paprika. Cook in preheated broiler 12 to 15 minutes, or until fish flakes easily. Makes 2 servings.

Oyster Stew

1 pint fresh shelled oysters
½ cup cold water
2 cups scalded milk
2 tablespoons butter
½ teaspoon salt

Empty oysters into a strainer over a large saucepan; pour cold water over oysters, allowing liquid to remain in saucepan. Remove any clinging bits of shell and add oysters to saucepan. Add scalded milk, butter, and salt; simmer 3 to 5 minutes, or until edges begin to curl. Serve at once with crackers. Makes 4 servings.

Banana Gelatin Cup

1 3-ounce package strawberry-flavored gelatin
1 cup boiling water
1 cup canned fruit syrup (drained from allowable fruit),
   or 1 cup cold water
1 ripe banana, sliced

Combine gelatin and boiling water; stir well until completely dissolved. Add fruit syrup and sliced banana. Pour into individual custard cups. Chill. Makes 4 servings.

Coffee Custard

3 tablespoons instant decaffeinated coffee
2 cups hot milk
3 eggs, slightly beaten
3 tablespoons sugar
½ teaspoon vanilla

Preheat oven to 350° F. Stir coffee into hot milk to dissolve. Mix eggs, sugar, and vanilla; add to coffee mixture and pour through strainer into custard cups. Place cups in a shallow pan and pour boiling water around the cups until cups are half submerged. Bake for 35 to 40 minutes, or until custard is firm. Cool and then chill. Makes 6 servings.

Bread Pudding Meringue

8 slices day-old seedless white bread
4 eggs, separated
¼ cup sugar
3 cups milk
1 teaspoon vanilla
3 tablespoons sugar

Preheat oven to 350° F. Cut bread into ½-inch cubes; place in a shallow buttered 1½-quart baking dish. Beat egg yolks with ¼ cup sugar, milk, and vanilla; pour over bread. Set baking dish in a pan containing 1 inch of hot water. Bake 40 minutes, or until center is firm to the touch. Remove dish from water and cool. Meanwhile, beat egg whites until foamy; beat in remaining sugar one tablespoon at a time until mixture forms stiff peaks. Spoon onto pudding, forming peaks here and there. Return to oven for 12 to 15 minutes, or until peaks are lightly browned. Makes 6 servings.

Orange Sponge Cake

4 eggs, separated
1 cup sugar
½ cup orange juice, strained
1 cup flour
1 teaspoon baking powder

Preheat oven to 325°F. Beat egg yolks until lemon-colored; add sugar and orange juice. Gradually add flour and baking powder. Beat whites separately until stiff peaks form. Fold the two mixtures together, mixing thoroughly; pour into an ungreased ring pan and bake 30 minutes, or until lightly browned. Makes 10 to 12 servings.

Sugar Cookies

2½ cups sifted flour
⅓ cup sugar
½ cup cold unsalted butter
1 teaspoon vanilla

Mix together flour and sugar; cut in butter and knead until smooth and firm. Add vanilla, working quickly to keep butter from melting. Chill for 1 hour. Preheat oven to 350° F. Roll dough on a floured board to ⅛-inch thickness and cut into 2-inch rounds. Place on greased cookie sheets and bake 10 to 15 minutes, or until lightly browned. Sprinkle with granulated sugar, if desired. Makes about 4 dozen cookies.

7

The Postgastrectomy Diet

After a partial stomach removal, called a gastrectomy, it's better to serve your patient many small meals than three large ones. This makes sense, as the gastrectomy obviously cuts the volume of the stomach, and too much food can cause discomfort and sometimes gagging or vomiting.

Your patient should eat very slowly and chew well, avoiding all very hot or very cold foods and drinks, all highly seasoned foods, and all fried foods. It's also a good idea to limit fluids with meals to prevent a bloated feeling, and to stay away from all alcoholic beverages and tobacco.

Ultimately, your patient will be able to resume a regular diet. Until then, with careful planning, this diet can be nutritionally adequate; it does not necessarily require the addition of supplemental vitamins.

	FOODS ALLOWED	**FOODS TO OMIT**
Beverages:	Milk, decaffeinated coffee, weak tea.	All others.
Eggs:	Omelet; scrambled, poached, soft-cooked, or hard-cooked—include 1 or more daily.	Fried eggs.
Fats:	Butter, light cream, heavy cream.	All others.
Cheese:	Cottage cheese, cream cheese; mild American cheese may be used in a sauce.	All others.
Breads and cereals:	White bread, day-old or toasted, white melba toast, zwieback, white crackers. Strained oatmeal, farina, cream of wheat.	All others.
Vegetables:	Pureed: asparagus, beets, carrots, peas, spinach, string beans, acorn squash, wax beans.	All others; all raw vegetables.

Fruit: Strained applesauce, strained prunes, cooked or canned pears, peaches, and apricots (without skins or seeds), baked apple (without skin or seeds).

All others.

Potato and substitutes: White potato, boiled, mashed, creamed, or baked (serve without skin). Macaroni, spaghetti, noodles, white rice.

All others.

Soup: Cream soups only, made with puree of vegetables.

All others.

Meat, fish, and poultry: Cut all meats fine and free of connective tissue: beef, lamb, veal, turkey, white meat of chicken, baked or boiled white fish.

All others.

Desserts: Soft custard, rennet puddings, rice pudding, plain puddings, fruit-flavored gelatin, vanilla ice cream (hold in mouth until partially melted), sponge cake, angel food cake.

All others and any containing nuts, coconut, or fruit.

Miscellaneous: Salt; limit sugar to 1 teaspoon daily.

All others.

SUGGESTED MENU PLAN

Breakfast
2 ounces orange juice
Cereal

Beverage
1 teaspoon sugar

Lunch
Strained cream soup
Minced fowl, fish, or meat
Potato or substitute
Pureed vegetable
Crackers
½ teaspoon butter

Dinner
Strained cream soup
Minced fowl, fish, or meat
Potato or substitute
Vegetable
½ slice white melba toast
½ teaspoon butter
½ cup milk

Mid-morning
Egg
½ slice dry white
    toast
½ teaspoon butter
½ cup milk

Early Afternoon
Bland fruit
White toast
½ teaspoon butter
½ cup milk

Late Afternoon
Dessert
½ cup milk

Bedtime
Fruit
White toast
½ teaspoon butter
½ cup milk

RECIPES

In addition to these recipes for a postgastrectomy diet the following recipes may also be used:

Eggs:
Carrot Soufflé 55
Cottage Cheese Omelet 117
Cracker Cheese Soufflé (omit nutmeg) 117
Hard-Cooked Eggs 30
Poached Eggs 31
Scrambled Cottage Cheese 30
Soft-Cooked Eggs 30

Vegetables:
Pureed Acorn Squash 62
Pureed Carrots (omit herbs) 58
Pureed Peas (omit herbs) 59
Pureed String Beans (omit herbs) 60
Pureed Wax Beans (omit herbs) 61

Potato and substitutes:
Cheesy Mashed Potatoes 62
Noodles and Cottage Cheese 63

Fruit:
Baked Apple 44

Soup:
Creamed Soup for Pureed Vegetables 21
Pureed Vegetables for Creamed Soup 20
Strained Cream Soup #1 56
Strained Cream Soup #2 56

Meat:
Filet Mignon Roast 120

Poultry:
>   Roast Turkey 64

Fish:
>   Halibut Mousse (omit nutmeg) 125
>   Poached Fish Rolls (omit dill) 65

Desserts:
>   Angel Food Cake 66
>   Snow Pudding 243
>   Soft Custard 22
>   Sponge Cake 245

Creamed Eggs on Toast

2 hard-cooked eggs
2 slices white toast
2 tablespoons butter
2 tablespoons flour
1 cup milk
¼ teaspoon salt

Slice eggs and place on toast. Melt butter in a saucepan; stir in flour until bubbly. Gradually stir in milk and cook until smooth and thick. Add salt. Pour over egg slices and serve. Makes 2 servings.

Eggs au Gratin

4 hard-cooked eggs
2 tablespoons butter
2 tablespoons flour
1 cup milk
¼ teaspoon salt
¼ cup grated mild American cheese
2 tablespoons toasted white bread crumbs

Preheat oven to 350° F. Cut eggs in half lengthwise and place in a buttered small baking dish. Melt butter in a saucepan. Stir in flour until thick and bubbly; stir in milk gradually until smooth and thick. Add salt. Pour over eggs, top with grated cheese, and sprinkle with bread crumbs. Bake for 15 minutes, or until cheese topping is melted. Makes 4 servings.

Squash Soufflé

1 acorn squash
2 eggs, separated
¼ teaspoon salt

Cut squash in half and scoop out seeds and membranes. Place cut halves down in a large skillet, add 1 inch of water, cover, and simmer until squash is fork-tender. Remove and scoop out of shell; place in electric blender with a little of the remaining water and blend until smooth. Preheat oven to 350°F. Beat egg yolks lightly and stir into 1 cup pureed squash; add salt. Beat egg whites until stiff peaks form and fold squash mixture carefully through whites. Spoon into a buttered baking dish. Bake 20 minutes, or until firm. Cut into serving portions. Makes 4 servings.

Baked Eggs in Potatoes

2 baking potatoes
2 teaspoons butter
½ teaspoon salt
2 eggs
1 tablespoon grated mild American cheese

Preheat oven to 350° F. Bake potatoes 45 minutes to 1 hour, until fork-tender. Cut off tops and scoop out potato; mash with butter and salt and return to skins. Make an indentation in each potato and break an egg into each. Sprinkle with cheese. Return to oven for 10 minutes, or until egg is cooked. Makes 2 servings.

NOTE: The patient should not eat the potato skin.

Pureed Asparagus on Pears

1 8-ounce can asparagus, with liquid
¼ teaspoon salt
1 teaspoon butter
1 8-ounce can pear halves, drained

Drain asparagus, reserving liquid. Place in an electric blender and add 2 tablespoons reserved liquid, salt, and butter and blend until completely pureed. Heat in the top of a double boiler over simmering water and spoon puree onto 2 pear halves for each serving. Makes 2 servings.

NOTE: Drained pear liquid can be added to gelatin in place of an equal amount of water. Remaining drained vegetable liquid can be refrigerated for use with other liquids and purees in preparing soup. For additional methods of pureeing vegetables, refer to Pureed Vegetables for Creamed Soup (see index).

Pureed Beets and Applesauce

1 8-ounce can sliced beets, with liquid
¼ teaspoon salt
1 teaspoon butter
¼ cup applesauce

Drain beets, reserving liquid. Place in an electric blender; add 2 tablespoons reserved liquid, salt, and butter and blend until completely pureed. Stir into applesauce. Heat in the top of a double boiler over simmering water. Makes 2 servings.

NOTE: For additional methods to puree vegetables, refer to Pureed Vegetables for Creamed Soup (see index).

Pureed Carrots on Peaches

1 8-ounce can sliced carrots, with liquid
¼ teaspoon salt
1 teaspoon butter
1 8-ounce can peach halves

Drain carrots, reserving liquid. Place in an electric blender; add 2 tablespoons reserved liquid, salt, and butter and blend until completely pureed. Heat in the top of a double boiler over simmering water. Spoon onto 2 peach halves for each serving. Makes 2 servings.

NOTE: Drained peach liquid can be added to gelatin in place of an equal amount of water. Remaining drained vegetable liquid can be refrigerated for use with other liquids and purees in preparing soup. For additional ways to puree vegetables, refer to Pureed Vegetables for Creamed Soup (see index).

Pureed Peas and Applesauce

1 8-ounce can peas, with liquid
¼ teaspoon salt
1 teaspoon butter
¼ cup applesauce

Drain peas, reserving liquid. Place in an electric blender; add 2 tablespoons reserved liquid, salt, and butter and blend until completely pureed. Stir into applesauce. Heat in the top of a double boiler over simmering water. Makes 2 servings.

NOTE: Remaining drained vegetable liquid can be refrigerated for use with other liquids and purees in preparing soup. For additional methods of pureeing vegetables, refer to Pureed Vegetables for Creamed Soup (see index).

Pureed Spinach on Pears

1 cup cooked spinach, with liquid
¼ teaspoon salt
1 teaspoon butter
1 8-ounce can pear halves, drained

Drain spinach, reserving liquid. Place spinach in an electric blender; add 2 tablespoons of the cooking liquid, salt, and butter and blend until completely pureed. Heat in the top of a double boiler over simmering water. Spoon onto 2 pear halves for each serving. Makes 2 servings.

NOTE: Drained pear liquid can be added to gelatin in place of an equal amount of water. Remaining liquid from cooked spinach can be refrigerated for use with other liquids and purees in preparing soup. For additional methods of pureeing vegetables, refer to Pureed Vegetables for Creamed Soup (see index).

Pureed Green Beans on Peaches

1 8-ounce can green beans, with liquid
¼ teaspoon salt
1 teaspoon butter
1 8-ounce can peach halves

Drain green beans, reserving liquid. Place in an electric blender; add 2 tablespoons liquid, salt, and butter and blend until completely pureed. Heat in the top of a double boiler over simmering water. Spoon onto 2 peach halves for each serving. Makes 2 servings.

NOTE: Drained peach liquid can be added to gelatin in place of an equal amount of water. Remaining drained vegetable liquid can be refrigerated for use with other liquids and purees in preparing soup. For additional ways to puree vegetables, refer to Pureed Vegetables for Creamed Soup (see index).

Pureed Wax Beans on Apricots

1 8-ounce can wax beans, with liquid
¼ teaspoon salt
1 teaspoon butter
1 8-ounce can peeled apricot halves

Drain wax beans, reserving liquid. Place in an electric blender; add 2 tablespoons reserved liquid, salt, and butter and blend until completely pureed. Heat in the top of a double boiler over simmering water. Spoon onto 2 apricot halves for each serving. Makes 2 servings.

NOTE: Drained apricot liquid can be added to gelatin in place of an equal amount of water. Remaining drained vegetable liquid can be refrigerated for use with other liquids and purees in preparing soup. For additional methods of pureeing vegetables, refer to Pureed Vegetables for Creamed Soup (see index).

Creamy Pureed Squash

1 small acorn squash
½ teaspoon salt
¼ cup light cream

Cut squash in half and scoop out seeds. Place in a saucepan, sprinkle with salt, and cover halfway with water. Cover pan and cook over low heat for 20 minutes, or until very tender. Remove from saucepan. Scoop squash out of shells into a bowl and mash with an electric beater, adding cream gradually. Makes 2 servings.

Creamy Mashed Potatoes

2 large potatoes, peeled and quartered
½ teaspoon salt
¼ cup light cream

Place potatoes into a small saucepan and cover with water. Add salt and cook for 20 minutes, or until very soft. Remove from water with a slotted spoon. Place in a small deep bowl and mash with an electric beater, gradually adding cream. Makes 2 servings.

Noodle Peach Bake

½ teaspoon salt
1 quart water
1 8-ounce package broad noodles
1 3-ounce package cream cheese
1 egg
1 8-ounce can sliced peaches, with syrup
Toasted white bread crumbs
2 tablespoons butter

Preheat oven to 350° F. Add salt to 1 quart water in a saucepan. Bring to a rapid boil and drop in noodles. Cook for 8 minutes. Drain. Mash cream cheese; add egg and mix well. Drain peaches; reserve syrup. Spoon in 2 tablespoons syrup, add peaches, and toss with cooked noodles. Spoon into a greased casserole, top with a thin layer of bread crumbs, and dot with butter. Bake 20 minutes, or until hot and lightly browned. Makes 4 servings.

Apricot Cheese Noodles

1 quart water
1 teaspoon salt
1 8-ounce package broad noodles
1 3-ounce package cream cheese
¼ cup milk
½ cup pureed apricots

Bring water to a boil and add salt. Add noodles and cook for 10 minutes, or until soft. Drain. Meanwhile, mash cream cheese with milk until smooth, adding additional milk if necessary to make a thick pliable sauce. Stir in apricots. Heat until warmed through; toss with noodles and serve. Makes 4 servings.

Spaghetti in Spinach Sauce

1 quart water
1 teaspoon salt
1 8-ounce package spaghetti
2 tablespoons butter
2 tablespoons flour
1 cup milk
½ teaspoon salt
½ cup pureed spinach (see index)

Bring water and salt to a boil; add spaghetti and cook for 10 minutes, or until soft. Meanwhile, melt butter in a saucepan; stir in flour and continue stirring until mixture is thick and bubbly. Gradually stir in milk, add salt, and continue to stir for several minutes until mixture is thickened. Stir in pureed spinach. Drain cooked spaghetti and toss with spinach sauce. Makes 4 servings.

NOTE: Extra spaghetti can be spooned into individual baking dishes and frozen. To reheat, thaw and bake at 350° F. for 20 minutes.

Baked Macaroni in Cheese Sauce

1 quart water
1 teaspoon salt
1 8-ounce package macaroni
1 cup light cream
3 slices mild American cheese, diced
¼ teaspoon salt
2 tablespoons toasted white bread crumbs
1 tablespoon butter

Preheat oven to 350° F. Bring water to a boil and add salt and macaroni; cook for 8 to 10 minutes, or until very tender. Drain. Meanwhile, heat cream in a small saucepan; add diced cheese and salt. Stir until cheese is completely melted. Remove from heat and toss through macaroni; spoon into a buttered baking dish or into individual baking dishes. Sprinkle with bread crumbs and dot with butter; bake 10 to 15 minutes. Makes 4 servings.

NOTE: If desired, bread crumbs and butter can be eliminated and macaroni can be served with the soft cheese sauce without baking. Extra portions can be frozen in individual baking dishes; to reheat, bring to room temperature and bake as directed above.

Apple Muffin Burgers

1 **pound lean ground beef**
1 **egg**
½ **cup applesauce**
½ **teaspoon salt**
1 **slice day-old white bread**

Preheat oven to 350° F. Combine ground beef, egg, applesauce, and salt. Wet slice of bread with water and tear into shreds; work into beef mixture. Spoon into a buttered muffin tin. Bake 20 to 25 minutes. Makes 6 servings.

Veal Balls in Apricot Sauce

1 **pound finely ground veal**
1 **egg**
½ **teaspoon salt**
1 **slice day-old white bread**
½ **cup water**
1 **cup pureed apricots**

Preheat oven to 350° F. Mix veal with egg and salt. Wet bread with water and crumble into veal; mix thoroughly and form into 1-inch balls. Place in a small baking dish and add ½ cup water. Pour in pureed apricots, coating veal balls well. Cover tightly and bake 45 minutes, or until tender. Makes 4 servings.

Potted Lamb Stew

1 **pound lean lamb cubes**
½ **cup water**
4 **carrots, scraped**
½ **pound string beans, trimmed**
4 **potatoes, peeled and quartered**
1 **teaspoon salt**

Preheat oven to 350° F. Place lamb cubes, trimmed of as much fat as possible, in a heavy Dutch oven or similar tightly lidded baking dish; add water. Cut carrots into chunks and add to pot; add whole beans, potatoes, and salt. Cover tightly and bake for 1 hour, adding additional water if necessary. Remove from oven. Cut up meat further, if necessary; force carrots, beans, and potatoes through a strainer, into separate piles on the plate. Top with butter, if desired. Makes 4 servings.

Poached Breast of Chicken

4 **halves of chicken breasts**
½ **teaspoon salt**
2 **cups water**
1 **teaspoon lemon juice**

Wash chicken parts and place in a large skillet. Sprinkle with salt; add water and lemon juice. Cover tightly and cook over low heat for 45 minutes. Remove chicken from skillet; do not use broth. Remove skin of cooked chicken. Makes 4 servings.

NOTE: Unused portions of poached chicken can be frozen in the cooking broth. To reheat, thaw and simmer until heated through; then proceed as above.

Peachy Broiled Chicken

4 halves of chicken breasts
½ teaspoon salt
2 tablespoons melted butter
½ cup pureed peaches

Arrange chicken breasts on a broiling pan, skin side up. Sprinkle with salt. Drizzle with melted butter. Broil in preheated broiler for 8 minutes; do not allow chicken skin to burn. Turn over and broil for an additional 8 minutes, or until chicken is cooked through. Remove chicken skin; turn again and spoon pureed peaches over chicken. Broil 3 to 4 more minutes and serve. Makes 4 servings.

Baked Chicken and Apricots

1 broiler chicken, cut up
½ teaspoon salt
1 tablespoon butter
1 8-ounce can peeled apricot halves

Preheat oven to 350° F. Arrange chicken parts in a small baking dish; sprinkle with salt and dot with butter. Place apricot halves on sheet with chicken and pour apricot liquid over them. Bake for 1 hour. Makes 4 servings.

Boiled Fish

1 pound filleted flounder, sole, or halibut
1 quart water
2 teaspoons lemon juice
1 carrot, scraped
1 teaspoon salt

Arrange fish slices in a large skillet; add water, lemon juice, carrot, and salt. Bring to a boil, then reduce heat to a simmer and cover skillet. Cook 10 minutes, or until fish flakes easily. Drain, discard carrot, and serve. Add additional salt, if desired. Makes 3 to 4 servings.

Broiled Flounder

2 slices fillet of flounder
¼ teaspoon salt
1 tablespoon butter
½ cup milk

Arrange flounder in a baking dish. Sprinkle with salt, dot with butter, and pour milk over fillets. Broil in preheated broiler 8 to 10 minutes, or until fish flakes easily. Makes 2 servings.

Applesauce

6 apples, cut up
1 cup water
¼ cup sugar
1 teaspoon lemon juice

Place cut-up apples, unpeeled and uncored, in a saucepan. Add water, sugar, and lemon juice. Cover and simmer for 20 minutes, or until apples are very soft. Work through a food mill to puree; remove skins and seeds. Makes 8 servings.

Poached Pears

1 cup water
¼ cup sugar
1 teaspoon lemon juice
6 fresh pears, peeled

Cook water and sugar together in a saucepan until sugar dissolves; add lemon juice. Add whole pears, setting upright with stems up. Cover and simmer until tender, about 15 to 20 minutes. Chill pears in syrup. Makes 6 servings.

NOTE: Bring pear to room temperature before serving, and serve with a minimum of syrup. If desired, cut pear in half, remove core, and serve with a dollop of whipped cream.

Prune Whip

¼ pound pitted prunes
1 teaspoon lemon juice
¼ cup sugar
2 egg whites

Place prunes in a small saucepan and cover with water; cook until soft. Remove prunes and puree in an electric blender or rub through a sieve. Discard cooking water. Return pureed prunes to saucepan. Add lemon juice and sugar and simmer, stirring constantly, until sugar is dissolved. Cool. Meanwhile preheat oven to 275° F. Beat egg whites until stiff and fold through cooled prunes. Spoon into buttered individual baking dishes and bake 25 to 30 minutes, or until firm. Cool and then chill until ready to serve. Makes 4 servings.

NOTE: Let Prune Whip come to room temperature before serving.

Gelatin Parfait

1 3-ounce package orange gelatin
1 3-ounce package lime gelatin
2 cups boiling water
2 cups cold water
½ cup pureed peaches
½ cup applesauce

Empty orange gelatin into one bowl and lime gelatin into another. Pour 1 cup boiling water into orange gelatin, stirring well to dissolve. Add 1 cup cold water and stir well; add pureed peaches. Then pour 1 cup boiling water into lime gelatin, and add cold water and applesauce. Chill. To serve, spoon layers of gelatin alternately into parfait glasses. Makes 8 servings.

Rice Cream

1 envelope (1 tablespoon) unflavored gelatin
1½ cups milk
1 3-ounce package cream cheese, softened
2 eggs, separated
3 tablespoons sugar
1 cup cooked white rice

Soften gelatin in ½ cup milk. Stir remaining milk into cream cheese and mix until smooth; add lightly beaten egg yolks and 2 tablespoons sugar. Stir in gelatin mixture and cook over low heat, stirring constantly, until mixture coats a spoon. Add rice and cool. Beat egg whites until frothy; add remaining tablespoon of sugar and beat until whites are stiff. Gently fold into rice mixture. Turn into a 1-quart mold, chill until firm, and cut into wedges. Makes 8 servings.

NOTE: Bring to room temperature before serving to patient.

Whipped Rice Pudding

1 cup white rice
1 cup water
½ teaspoon salt
2½ cups milk
2 tablespoons sugar
1 tablespoon butter
½ pint heavy cream, whipped

Combine rice, water, and salt in the top of a double boiler. Cook over direct heat for 5 minutes. Stir in milk and sugar and heat to boiling; then place over boiling water, cover, and continue cooking about 25 minutes, or until all liquid is absorbed. Remove from heat. Stir in butter and fluff rice; cool. Fold in whipped cream and spoon into dessert dishes. Makes 8 servings.

Baked Rice Pudding

½ cup white rice
1 quart milk
¼ cup sugar
⅛ teaspoon salt

Preheat oven to 325°F. Combine rice, milk, sugar, and salt. Pour into a buttered casserole; cover. Bake about 2 hours, or until rice has softened. Remove cover and bake a few minutes longer. Serve with whipped cream, if desired. Makes 8 servings.

8

The Low-Residue Diet

This diet is often used postoperatively when roughage and bulk in the digestive tract must be kept to a minimum. It's particularly recommended after an ileostomy to keep a soothing flow of food through the tender areas.

There are times when your doctor may order a variation of this moderate diet, the Minimal-Residue Diet. This can be done by omitting the milk and potato allowed on the regular Low-Residue Diet and pureeing all allowed vegetables and fruits.

The Low-Residue Diet is nutritionally adequate and does not necessarily require additional vitamin supplements if you plan your menus carefully. But the Minimal-Residue Diet is deficient in calcium, because of the lack of milk in the diet, and requires supplemental calcium if it will be used over a long period of time.

	FOODS ALLOWED	**FOODS TO OMIT**
Beverages:	Milk, milk beverages, buttermilk—limit to 2 cups daily. Coffee, tea, pure cocoa, carbonated beverages.	Alcoholic beverages.
Eggs:	Omelet; scrambled, poached, soft-cooked, or hard-cooked—include 1 or more daily.	Fried eggs.
Fats:	Butter, light cream, heavy cream, salad oil, margarine.	All others.
Cheese:	Cream cheese, cottage cheese, mild American cheese.	All others.
Breads and cereals:	White or rye bread without seeds (day-old or toasted); white rolls (dried or toasted); white melba toast, saltines, soda crackers, zwieback, matzoh—include 2 to 4 slices of bread daily. Cooked cereals: enriched fine white cereal or well-cooked strained oatmeal. Dry cereals; corn or rice flakes, puffed rice—include 1 serving of any cereal daily.	Graham crackers, hot breads, biscuits, whole-grain breads, seeded bread and rolls, bran, coarse cereals, rye bread with seeds, pumpernickel, all other cereals.

Vegetables:	Canned or cooked asparagus tips, carrots, beets, pureed peas, spinach, Swiss chard, wax beans, string beans, winter squash and tomato juice—include 3 to 4 servings daily, with at least 1 green and 1 yellow.	All others, including broccoli, brussels sprouts, cabbage, cauliflower, celery, onions, parsnips, summer squash, turnips, lima beans, dried peas and beans.
Fruit:	Strained fruit juice, ripe bananas, cooked or canned applesauce; peeled apricots, peaches, and pears (no seeds or skins)—include 1 to 2 servings of fruit and 1 serving of citrus juice daily.	Raw fruits except ripe bananas; cooked or canned berries, cherries, pineapple; raisins; all cooked fruit with seeds and skins.
Potato and substitutes:	White potato, creamed, mashed, boiled, or baked, served with no skin. Macaroni, spaghetti, noodles, white rice. Include 1 potato daily.	Fried potatoes, roasted potatoes, potato chips, brown rice, white rice, sweet potatoes, yams.
Soup:	Strained cream soups made with part of allowed milk and vegetables. Broth with vegetables or pasta.	All soups made with nonallowed vegetables.

Meat, fish and poultry:	Ground beef; tender cuts of beef, veal, lamb; liver, sweet-breads; chicken or turkey without skin; white-flesh fish, canned tuna and salmon. All meat must be tender and free of coarse connec-tive fibers; include 2 servings daily, and liver once a week.	Duck, goose, fried meats, lobster, crabmeat, shrimp, smoked and spiced meats and fish, all other fish.
Desserts:	Sponge cake, angel food cake, plain sugar wafers, vanilla wafers, custard, plain puddings, rennet cus-tards, fruit-flavored gelatin, plain ice cream, water ices, and sherbets.	Pies, pastry, and desserts containing nuts, coconut, and nonallowed fruits.
Miscellaneous:	Salt, sugar, honey, paprika, oregano, cinnamon, nutmeg, rosemary, basil, dill, vanilla, limited amounts of white sauce, vinegar, cream-style peanut butter, pure cocoa, chocolate, and jelly.	All other condi-ments, garlic, pickles, pepper, ginger, seed spices, mace, parsley, mint, mustard, horseradish, olives, salad dressings, nuts, coconut, jam, gravy, chili powder, and cocoa mixes.

SUGGESTED MENU PLAN

Breakfast
Fruit juice
Cereal
Egg
White toast
Butter
Beverage
*½ cup milk

Lunch
Meat, fish, or poultry
*Potato or substitute
Vegetable
Fruit
Bread
Butter
Beverage
*½ cup milk

Dinner
Meat, fish, poultry, or eggs
*Potato or substitute
Vegetable
Dessert or fruit
Bread
Butter
Beverage
*½ cup milk

*For Minimal-Residue Diet, eliminate milk and potato.

RECIPES

In addition to these recipes for the Low-Residue Diet, the following recipes may also be used:

Beverages:
Eggnog 19
Orange Eggnog 19

Eggs:
Baked Egg Florentine 32
*Baked Eggs in Potatoes 93
Carrot Soufflé 55
Cheese Omelet 31
Creamed Eggs on Toast 91
Eggs au Gratin 92
Grape Soufflé 74
Hard-Cooked Eggs 30
Peanut Butter Omelet 55
Poached Eggs 31
Scrambled Cottage Cheese 30
Soft-Cooked Eggs 30
Spinach Soufflé 38
Squash Soufflé 92

Vegetables:
Asparagus with Blender Hollandaise 35
Baked Acorn Squash 37
Boiled Beets 36
Carrot Strips 74
Creamy Pureed Squash 97
Easy Creamed Spinach 38
Green Beans in Tomato Sauce 39
Harvard Beets #2 230
Honeyed Carrots 37
**Pureed Acorn Squash 62
**Pureed Asparagus on Pears 93

Soup:

    Chicken Broth 33
    Cold Borscht 209
    Cream of Asparagus Soup 230
    Cream of Chicken Soup 21
    Creamed Soup for Pureed Vegetables 21
  *Dilled Potato Soup 34
    Pureed Vegetables for Creamed Soup 20
    Quick Asparagus Soup 35
    Strained Cream Soup #1 56
    Strained Cream Soup #2 56

Meat:

    Apple Muffin Burgers 101
    Baked Beef Stew 42
    Baked Breaded Sweetbreads 80
    Baked Veal Chops 217
    Broiled Calf Liver 79
  *Fluffy Meat Loaf 41
    Potted Lamb Stew 102
    Veal Balls in Apricot Sauce 101
    Veal Stew 79

Poultry:

    Apricot Jellied Turkey Roll 64
    Baked Chicken and Apricots 103
    Baked Chicken with Peaches 80
    Baked Orange Chicken 43
    Broiled Tarragon Chicken 82
    Chicken Livers Oregano 81
    Chopped Liver and Bean Spread 82
    Orange Glazed Chicken 218
    Peachy Baked Chicken 217
    Peachy Broiled Chicken 103
    Poached Breast of Chicken 102
    Roast Turkey 64

*Omit for Minimal-Residue Diet
**Use for Minimal-Residue Diet

Cottage Cheese Omelet

2 eggs
1 tablespoon cold water
2 tablespoons butter
¼ cup cold cottage cheese

Beat eggs and water together. Melt butter in a small skillet; pour in beaten eggs. As edges cook, lift to let liquid egg run out to the edges. While still moist, turn out onto plate. Spoon cottage cheese over half the omelet and fold to cover filling. Makes 1 serving.

Cracker Cheese Soufflé

10 saltine crackers
1½ cups milk
¼ cup grated mild American cheese
⅛ teaspoon salt
Dash nutmeg
3 eggs, separated

Break crackers into a bowl; add milk and let stand about 1 hour. Stir until smooth. Add cheese, salt, and nutmeg; beat egg yolks slightly and add to milk mixture. Preheat oven to 325° F. Beat egg whites until stiff peaks form; fold into milk mixture. Pour into a 1-quart soufflé dish and bake about 40 minutes. Makes 6 servings.

Spinach and Egg Casserole

1 10-ounce package frozen chopped spinach
1 cup water
¼ teaspoon salt
⅛ teaspoon nutmeg
1 tablespoon butter
1 tablespoon flour
1 cup milk
1 tablespoon grated mild American cheese
4 eggs

Preheat oven to 325°F. Place spinach in a small saucepan; add water, salt, and nutmeg. Cook until soft; drain. Spoon into a small buttered flat baking dish. Melt butter in a small saucepan; stir in flour and then gradually stir in milk. Cook over low heat, stirring constantly, until mixture is bubbly and thick. Stir in cheese. Break eggs over spinach; spoon cheese sauce over eggs. Bake 20 to 25 minutes, or until eggs are cooked as desired. Makes 4 servings.

Shredded Carrots

2 tablespoons butter
4 cups shredded carrots
½ teaspoon salt
½ cup water
1 tablespoon lemon juice
1 teaspoon sugar

Melt butter in a saucepan; add carrots and salt. Combine water, lemon juice, and sugar; pour over carrots. Cover and cook over low heat for 15 minutes, or until very tender. Makes 4 servings.

Green Beans Oregano

1 10-ounce package frozen green beans
1 cup tomato juice
¼ teaspoon salt
⅛ teaspoon oregano

Place green beans in a saucepan and add tomato juice, salt, and oregano. Cover and simmer, stirring occasionally, 10 minutes, or until beans are soft. Makes 4 servings.

Dilled Pureed Peas

1 pound fresh peas, *or*
  1 10-ounce package frozen peas, *or*
  1 16-ounce can peas
½ teaspoon sugar
½ teaspoon salt
¼ teaspoon dried dillweed
1 teaspoon butter

Shell fresh peas. Place fresh or frozen peas in a saucepan and cover with water. Add sugar, salt, and dillweed; cook 15 to 20 minutes, or until very tender. If using canned peas, add sugar and dill and heat. Drain. Force peas through a strainer or food mill; stir in butter. Serve in an attractive dish; surround with cooked carrots if desired. Makes 4 servings.

NOTE: Leftover pureed vegetables can be refrigerated in tightly closed containers for 2 days. Remaining liquid can be used to flavor cream soup, by boiling and reducing in volume first.

Rice and Carrot Ring

1 **cup cooked white rice**
1 **cup grated carrots, cooked**
1 **cup grated mild American cheese**
2 **eggs, beaten**
½ **teaspoon salt**

Preheat oven to 350°F. Combine rice and carrots. Add cheese and stir in beaten eggs and salt. Spoon into a greased 1-quart ring mold. Place in a pan of hot water and bake 20 minutes. Makes 6 servings.

Filet Mignon Roast

½ **piece filet mignon, about 2 pounds,**
    preferably the front end
½ **teaspoon salt**
½ **teaspoon paprika**
½ **cup water**

Preheat oven to 450°F. Place filet mignon roast in a small baking pan; season with salt and paprika. Pour water into pan and bake 20 minutes for rare, 25 minutes for medium-done. Remove from oven and let stand 10 minutes, then slice and serve. Makes 6 servings.

Macaroni with Meat Sauce

1 pound lean ground beef
1 can tomato paste
1 cup water
½ teaspoon salt
¼ teaspoon oregano
1 8-ounce package macaroni, cooked
2 slices mild American cheese, diced (optional)

Crumble ground beef into a large skillet. Cook and break beef apart into smaller bits, keeping mixture moving so it doesn't burn. When browned, add tomato paste mixed with water, salt, and oregano. Cook, covered, 10 minutes. Stir in macaroni and diced cheese. Cook several minutes longer. Makes 6 servings.

Meat Loaf with Peach Sauce

1 pound lean ground beef
1 egg
½ cup tomato juice
1 slice white bread
½ teaspoon salt
¼ teaspoon oregano
1 16-ounce can peach slices, with juice
½ teaspoon cornstarch
⅛ teaspoon nutmeg

Preheat oven to 350°F. Combine ground beef and egg. Pour tomato juice over white bread slice in a bowl, crumble bread into fine pieces, and add to beef. Add salt and oregano and mix well. Spoon into a greased loaf pan and bake for 1 hour. 20 minutes before meat loaf is done, drain peach slices and pour ½ cup juice into a saucepan; stir in cornstarch and nutmeg until completely dissolved. Heat and stir constantly until mixture thickens and boils. Add peach slices and heat for several minutes. Pour mixture over meat loaf about 10 minutes before it's done. Makes 4 to 6 servings.

Leg of Lamb Roast

2 tablespoons dark brown sugar
2 tablespoons salad oil
½ leg of lamb roast, shank end
1½ cups tomato juice
1 teaspoon oregano
½ teaspoon salt

Preheat oven to 425°F. Stir brown sugar into oil and rub over lamb. Place roast in a baking pan. Combine tomato juice, oregano, and salt; pour over roast. Roast 15 minutes, then reduce heat to 350° and bake for one hour, basting occasionally with pan juices. Makes 4 to 6 servings.

Veal Chops Rosemary

4 tablespoons butter or margarine
4 rib veal chops
¼ cup flour
½ teaspoon salt
¼ teaspoon paprika
1 cup tomato juice
½ teaspoon dried rosemary
Lemon slices

Melt butter in a large skillet. Shake veal chops in a plastic bag with flour, salt, and paprika; shake off excess and lightly brown in butter, turning to brown both sides. Pour tomato juice around chops and sprinkle with rosemary; cover and simmer 20 minutes, or until chops are tender. Serve with lemon slices. Makes 4 servings.

Chicken Stroganoff

1 broiler chicken, cut up
¼ cup lemon juice
¼ cup butter or margarine
½ teaspoon salt
½ teaspoon paprika
½ cup water
¼ cup dairy sour cream

Sprinkle chicken with lemon juice and refrigerate for one hour. Then melt butter in a heavy skillet; brown chicken on all sides. Sprinkle with salt and paprika. Add water and cover tightly; cook over low heat for 45 minutes, or until fork-tender. Remove chicken to a platter. Stir sour cream into remaining broth, cooking over very low heat to prevent curdling. Pour over chicken and serve. Dash paprika over chicken, if desired. Makes 4 servings.

Chicken Tetrazzini

1 tablespoon butter
1 tablespoon flour
1 cup milk
¼ teaspoon salt
¼ teaspoon paprika
1 teaspoon lemon juice
2 cups cooked cubed chicken
1 8-ounce package broad noodles, cooked
¼ cup crumbs from white toast
2 tablespoons butter

Preheat oven to 400°F. Melt 1 tablespoon butter in a saucepan. Stir in flour and cook until bubbly; gradually stir in milk and cook and stir constantly until mixture thickens. Add salt, paprika, and lemon juice. Combine sauce with cooked chicken and noodles; spoon into a buttered baking dish, top with crumbs, and dot with butter. Bake 15 minutes, or until crumbs are browned and ingredients are bubbly. Makes 4 servings.

Baked Chicken Stew

1 broiler chicken
2 cups chicken broth (may be made with bouillon cubes)
2 tablespoons tomato paste
2 sprigs fresh dillweed
½ teaspoon salt
½ teaspoon sugar
¼ teaspoon paprika
8 whole carrots, scraped
4 potatoes, peeled and quartered
1 10-ounce package frozen green beans

Preheat oven to 350°F. Place whole chicken in a Dutch oven or heavy covered casserole. Add chicken broth mixed with tomato paste, dill, salt, sugar, and paprika. Cut carrots into large chunks and add with potatoes. Bake 1 hour, covered; add green beans 15 minutes before chicken is completely cooked. Makes 4 servings.

Halibut Mousse

1 cup light cream
2 cups bread crumbs from white bread
1 pound raw halibut, ground or chopped fine
1 teaspoon salt
⅛ teaspoon nutmeg
4 egg whites

Preheat oven to 350°F. Stir cream into bread crumbs; add ground halibut, salt, and nutmeg. Beat egg whites until stiff; fold into fish mixture. Spoon into a greased loaf pan. Place the pan in a larger pan of hot water. Bake 45 minutes, or until firm. Let stand 10 minutes before slicing. Makes 6 servings.

Poached Haddock

2 pounds thick haddock fillets
½ teaspoon salt
1 sprig dillweed
1 tablespoon vinegar
Lemon slices
Dash paprika

Arrange haddock slices in a large skillet and cover with water.
Add salt, dill, and vinegar; bring to a boil, then reduce heat and
simmer 10 minutes, or until fish flakes easily. Carefully remove
fish slices from skillet with a large spatula and place on a serving platter. Garnish with lemon slices and a dash of paprika.
Makes 4 to 6 servings.

Tuna Cheese Casserole

½ cup butter
1 cup light cream
1 8-ounce package cream cheese
1 8-ounce package broad noodles, cooked
2 7½-ounce cans tuna, drained
½ teaspoon salt
½ teaspoon dried dillweed

Preheat oven to 350°F. Melt butter in a saucepan; add cream
and cream cheese and cook until cheese is melted and ingredients are well blended. Add cooked noodles, flaked tuna, salt, and
dill. Spoon into a greased casserole and bake 20 minutes, or until bubbling. Makes 4 servings.

Tuna Lasagna

2 cups tomato juice
2 tablespoons tomato paste
1 teaspoon oregano
1 teaspoon sugar
2 7-ounce cans tuna, drained
8 ounces lasagna noodles
1½ cups cottage cheese
1 egg
2 tablespoons grated American cheese

Combine tomato juice, tomato paste, oregano, and sugar in a saucepan; simmer 5 minutes, stirring occasionally. Add flaked tuna. Meanwhile, cook lasagna noodles according to package directions. Preheat oven to 350° F. Place half the cooked and drained lasagna noodles in a single layer in a buttered shallow 2-quart baking dish. Cover with one-third of tuna sauce. Combine cottage cheese and egg; spread half the mixture in a layer over tuna sauce in baking dish. Repeat layers, ending with a top layer of tuna sauce. Sprinkle grated American cheese over top. Bake 30 minutes; let stand 15 minutes before cutting into squares for serving. Makes 6 to 8 servings.

Chocolate Cake

½ cup butter
1½ cups sugar
4 eggs, separated
1 teaspoon vanilla
2 squares unsweetened baking chocolate
5 tablespoons water
1¾ cups sifted flour
2 teaspoons baking powder
½ cup milk

Preheat oven to 350°F. Beat butter and gradually add sugar; beat until light and fluffy. Add egg yolks, one at a time, and vanilla. In a small saucepan, melt baking chocolate in water, stirring just until melted and smooth; add to creamed mixture. Sift together flour and baking powder and add to creamed mixture alternately with milk, beginning and ending with dry ingredients. Beat egg whites to soft peak stage; fold into chocolate batter. Pour into a greased tube pan and bake 30 to 35 minutes. Remove and cool. Makes 12 servings.

Crustless Orange Cheese Pie

1 envelope (1 tablespoon) unflavored gelatin
2 tablespoons water
½ cup sugar
1 egg, separated
½ cup frozen concentrated orange juice, thawed
1½ cups cottage cheese
½ cup heavy cream, whipped
2 tablespoons sugar

Soften gelatin in water and set aside. In a large saucepan, combine ½ cup sugar, egg yolk, and orange juice; cook over medium heat, stirring constantly, until thickened. Remove from heat, add softened gelatin, and stir until well blended. Cool. In a large mixing bowl, beat cottage cheese until smooth; stir in gelatin mixture and fold in whipped cream. Beat egg white until foamy; gradually add 2 tablespoons sugar and beat until stiff. Fold into cottage cheese mixture and spoon into a 9-inch pie plate. Chill. Garnish with canned peeled sliced peaches, if desired. Makes 8 servings.

Lime Pie

⅓ cup butter
¼ cup sugar
2 tablespoons unsweetened cocoa
1 cup corn flake crumbs
2 3-ounce packages lime-flavored gelatin
2½ cups boiling water
1 pint heavy cream

Combine butter, sugar, and cocoa in a small saucepan. Cook over low heat, stirring constantly, until mixture boils. Remove from heat and add corn flake crumbs, mixing well. Press crumb mixture into the bottom and sides of a 9-inch pie pan to form a thin crust. Chill. Dissolve one package of gelatin in 1½ cups of boiling water; pour into an 8-inch square pan and chill. Dissolve the other package of gelatin in the remaining cup of boiling water; chill to the consistency of unbeaten egg whites. Whip until foamy and doubled in volume. Cut pan of firm gelatin into cubes. Whip cream; fold whipped gelatin and gelatin cubes into whipped cream. Spoon into prepared crust and chill for at least 1 hour, or until firm. Makes 8 servings.

9

The High-Residue Diet

This diet is often prescribed when a doctor sees a need to keep a large amount of roughage and bulk in the digestive tract to keep the bowel in active working order. Proctologists favor this type of regime to keep the intestine constantly stimulated, and to aid in evacuation of the colon. It's easy to follow this routine if bran and whole-wheat products are added to a normal diet, along with all vegetables of the cabbage family.

Foods to avoid are refined grains, including cereals like farina and all forms of pasta. Fried foods are also omitted, along with other greasy foods and pastries, pies, and cakes.

This is a very healthy regime for those without delicate digestive problems, and can easily be planned to be nutritionally adequate without any vitamin supplements.

130

	FOODS ALLOWED	**FOODS TO OMIT**
Beverages:	Milk, milk beverages, buttermilk, coffee, tea, cocoa, carbonated beverages.	None.
Eggs:	Omelet; scrambled, poached, soft-cooked, or hard-cooked—include 1 or more daily.	Fried eggs.
Fats:	Butter, cream, olive oil, salad dressings.	None.
Cheese:	All types.	None.
Breads and cereals:	Whole wheat, cracked wheat, rye, and pumpernickel breads. Oatmeal, whole-wheat cooked cereals. Dry cereals: bran, whole wheat, puffed wheat.	White bread, cream of wheat, farina, and other highly refined cereals; puffed rice.
Vegetables:	Asparagus, broccoli, brussels sprouts, carrots, cabbage, cauliflower, celery, corn, eggplant, lettuce, lima beans, onions, peas, peppers,	None.

	radishes, sauer-kraut, spinach, string beans, Swiss chard, squash (all types), and tomatoes.	
Fruit:	All, including skins.	None.
Potato and substitutes:	All potatoes and sweet potatoes, except fried; whole-grain rice.	Fried potatoes, white rice, macaroni, spaghetti, noodles.
Soup:	All kinds.	None.
Meat, fish, and poultry:	All kinds, except fried.	Everything fried.
Desserts:	All except pastries, cakes, and pies.	Pastries, cakes, and pies.
Miscellaneous:	All seasonings.	Greasy food and nuts.

SUGGESTED MENU PLAN

Breakfast
Fruit juice
Bran cereal
Egg
Whole-wheat bread
Butter
Beverage
Milk

Lunch	**Dinner**
Meat, fish, or poultry	Meat, fish, poultry, or eggs
Potato	Potato or substitute
Vegetable	Vegetable
Fresh fruit	Dessert
Whole-wheat bread	Bread
Butter	Butter
Beverage	Milk
Milk	Beverage

RECIPES

In combination with the recipes for the High-Residue Diet, the following recipes may also be used:

Beverages:
    Double Milk Eggnog   54
    Eggnog   19
    Orange Eggnog   19
    Slim Skimnog   54

Eggs:
    Baked Egg Florentine   32
    Cheese Omelet   31
    Cottage Cheese Omelet   208
    Grape Soufflé   74
    Hard-Cooked Eggs   30
    Poached Eggs   31
    Scrambled Cottage Cheese   30
    Soft-Cooked Eggs   30
    Spanish Omelet   208
    Spinach and Egg Casserole   118

Meat:

 Baked Beef Stew 42
 Baked Breaded Sweetbreads 80
 Baked Swiss Steak 236
 Broiled Calf Liver 79
 Filet Mignon Roast 120
 Leg of Lamb Roast 122
 Potted Lamb Stew 102
 Swedish Meat Balls 235
 Veal Chops Rosemary 122
 Veal Stew 79

Poultry:

 Apricot Jellied Turkey Roll 64
 Baked Chicken and Apricots 103
 Baked Chicken Stew 125
 Baked Chicken with Peaches 80
 Baked Chicken with Pineapple-Cheese Sauce 237
 Baked Orange Chicken 43
 Broiled Tarragon Chicken 82
 Chicken Livers Oregano 81
 Chicken Stroganoff 123
 Chopped Liver and Bean Spread 82
 Orange Glazed Chicken 218
 Peachy Baked Chicken 217
 Poached Breast of Chicken 102
 Roast Turkey 64

Cabbage Soup

1 pound beef neck bones
1½ quarts water
1 teaspoon salt
1 medium head cabbage, shredded
2 onions, sliced
1 potato, peeled and diced
1 29-ounce can tomatoes packed in sauce
¼ cup white seedless raisins
¼ cup lemon juice
2 tablespoons brown sugar
1 bay leaf
½ teaspoon pepper

Place neck bones, water, and salt in a large deep pot, and bring
to a boil. Skim surface with a large spoon to remove residue.
Lower heat and add cabbage, onions, potato, tomatoes, raisins,
lemon juice, brown sugar, bay leaf, and pepper; simmer several
hours. Taste and add additional lemon juice or sugar as needed
for a balanced sweet and sour taste. Makes 8 servings.

Sauerkraut Soup

2 pounds fresh sauerkraut
1 29-ounce can tomatoes
3 onions, sliced
2 tablespoons butter or margarine
1 pound beef neck bones
1 teaspoon salt
1½ teaspoons pepper
2 tablespoons brown sugar

Combine sauerkraut and tomatoes in a large pot. Sauté onions in butter in a large skillet until golden brown; add to the sauerkraut. Add beef bones, salt, pepper, and brown sugar. Cover with water. Bring to a boil, then reduce heat; cover pot and simmer for 3 hours, skimming and stirring occasionally. Makes 8 servings.

Broccoli Soufflé

1 10-ounce package frozen chopped broccoli
2 tablespoons butter
2 tablespoons flour
1 cup milk
½ teaspoon salt
⅛ teaspoon nutmeg
¼ cup finely grated Parmesan cheese
4 eggs, separated

Preheat oven to 350°F. Cook chopped broccoli according to package directions and drain thoroughly. In a saucepan, melt butter; stir in flour until it thickens and add milk gradually, stirring constantly. Add salt and nutmeg and stir in cheese. Remove from heat and stir in slightly beaten egg yolks. Beat egg whites until stiff peaks form. Fold the two mixtures together and spoon into a 1-quart ungreased soufflé dish; bake 35 minutes, or until lightly browned. Serve at once. Makes 4 servings.

Broccoli with Orange Sauce

2 10-ounce packages frozen broccoli
1 cup sour cream
2 tablespoons frozen concentrated orange juice
½ teaspoon salt
⅛ teaspoon nutmeg

Cook broccoli as directed on package, until tender. Combine sour cream, orange juice concentrate, salt, and nutmeg in a small saucepan; stir over low heat until smooth and hot, but do not boil. Drain cooked broccoli, cover with sauce and serve. Makes 6 servings.

Brussels Sprouts

1 10-ounce package frozen brussels sprouts
1 cup water
½ teaspoon salt
½ teaspoon sugar
⅛ teaspoon pepper
1 tablespoon butter
1 teaspoon lemon juice
1 teaspoon chopped parsley

Cut sprouts in half lengthwise and place in a saucepan with water, salt, sugar, and pepper. Cook 5 minutes, or until sprouts are tender but not mushy. Drain. Add butter, lemon juice, and parsley; toss lightly and serve. Makes 4 servings.

Cauliflower with Cheddar Sauce

1 large head cauliflower
½ teaspoon salt
2 tablespoons butter
2 tablespoons flour
1 cup milk
¼ cup grated Cheddar cheese
¼ teaspoon salt
⅛ teaspoon pepper
Dash paprika

Wash cauliflower thoroughly. Place in a saucepan, head up; sprinkle with salt and add 1 inch of water to pan. Cover and cook 15 to 20 minutes, or until tender; drain well and place on a platter. Meanwhile, melt butter in a small saucepan; stir in flour until thick and bubbly. Add milk and then cheese, salt, and pepper. Stirring constantly, cook until entire mixture is thick and bubbly. Pour over hot cooked cauliflower. Dash paprika lightly over top. Makes 6 servings.

Baked Cauliflower

1 large head cauliflower
1 onion, diced
2 tablespoons chopped parsley
1 clove garlic, minced
1 16-ounce can stewed tomatoes
½ teaspoon salt
¼ teaspoon pepper
¼ cup grated Parmesan cheese

Preheat oven to 350°F. Wash cauliflower and break into small flowerets. In a covered casserole, combine onion, parsley, garlic, and tomatoes; add salt, pepper, and grated cheese. Add cauliflowerets and mix thoroughly. Cover and bake 40 minutes, or until cauliflower is tender. Makes 6 servings.

Lemon-Buttered Cabbage

¼ cup butter
1 large head cabbage, shredded
¼ cup lemon juice
½ teaspoon celery seed
½ teaspoon salt
⅛ teaspoon pepper

Melt butter in a large skillet. Add shredded cabbage, lemon juice, celery seed, salt, and pepper. Cover and cook, stirring occasionally, 10 minutes, or until tender. Makes 6 servings.

Cabbage Salad

1 large head cabbage, shredded
1 small onion, sliced paper-thin
1 green pepper, sliced thin
2 carrots, grated
½ teaspoon celery seed
¼ cup wine vinegar
¼ cup sugar
1 cup water

Combine shredded cabbage, onion, pepper, carrots, and celery seed. Stir wine vinegar and sugar into water; pour over salad. Cover tightly and refrigerate several hours before serving. Makes 6 to 8 servings.

Coleslaw

1 head cabbage, shredded
1 green pepper, sliced thin
4 carrots, grated
½ cup mayonnaise
½ cup dairy sour cream
¼ cup wine vinegar
1 tablespoon sugar
½ teaspoon salt
⅛ teaspoon pepper

Combine cabbage, green pepper, and carrots in a large bowl. Mix together mayonnaise, sour cream, and vinegar; stir in sugar, salt, and pepper. Pour dressing over cabbage and toss lightly to coat well. Refrigerate several hours before serving. Makes 6 to 8 servings.

Sweet and Sour Red Cabbage

1 medium head red cabbage, shredded
1½ cups water
2 tablespoons brown sugar
2 tablespoons lemon juice
1 tablespoon wine vinegar
2 whole cloves
½ teaspoon ginger
½ teaspoon salt

Place shredded cabbage in a deep saucepan. Add water, brown sugar, lemon juice, wine vinegar, cloves, ginger, and salt; stir well. Cover and simmer 35 minutes, or until cabbage is tender. Makes 6 to 8 servings.

Baked Wild Rice

¼ cup salad oil
1 onion, diced
1 green pepper, diced
2 cups wild rice
5 cups chicken broth
    (may be made from bouillon cubes)
½ teaspoon salt
⅛ teaspoon pepper

Preheat oven to 275°F. Heat oil in a skillet; sauté onion and green pepper until limp. Add wild rice and stir until golden. Empty into a casserole with a tight cover; stir in chicken broth, salt, and pepper. Cover and bake 1 hour, or until all liquid is absorbed. Fluff rice with a fork and serve. Makes 8 servings.

Wild Rice and Mushroom Ring

1 cup wild rice
1 teaspoon salt
1 quart water
1 pound mushrooms, chopped
3 tablespoons butter
2 tablespoons chopped parsley

Wash rice thoroughly. Boil in salted water for 45 minutes; drain. Preheat oven to 350°F. Sauté mushrooms in butter until limp; add to rice. Add parsley. Pour into a greased 1-quart ring mold and set in a pan of hot water; bake 30 minutes. Turn out onto a platter and fill center with cooked vegetables, if desired. Makes 6 servings.

Meat Loaf

2 pounds ground beef
1 egg
½ cup raw oatmeal
1 onion, grated
¼ cup chopped parsley
½ cup tomato juice
1 teaspoon salt
¼ teaspoon pepper
1 8-ounce can tomato sauce

Preheat oven to 350°F. Combine beef, egg, oatmeal, onion, and parsley; stir in tomato juice, salt, and pepper and mix well. Spoon into a loaf pan, pressing to shape firmly. Top with tomato sauce and bake 1 hour. Makes 6 to 8 servings.

Sweet and Sour Brisket

4-pound brisket of beef
1 pound sauerkraut
1 16-ounce can tomato sauce
3 apples, peeled and sliced
2 onions, sliced
2 tablespoons brown sugar
Juice of 2 lemons
½ teaspoon salt
¼ teaspoon pepper

Place beef in a large Dutch oven or similar covered pot. Combine sauerkraut, tomato sauce, apples, onions, brown sugar, lemon juice, salt, and pepper; pour around the brisket. Cover and simmer 2½ hours, adding water if necessary to keep from sticking. Taste and add more lemon juice or sugar to get a balanced flavor. Serve slices with gravy. Makes 8 servings.

Stuffed Cabbage

1 large head cabbage
2 pounds lean ground beef
1 onion, grated
1 apple, grated
½ cup whole-grain rice
½ teaspoon salt
¼ teaspoon pepper
½ cup water
1 29-ounce can tomatoes
1 onion, sliced
½ cup brown sugar
¼ cup lemon juice
½ teaspoon salt
½ teaspoon ground ginger

Parboil cabbage. Cut around the core and carefully remove leaves one by one; trim heavy center lines where necessary. Combine beef, grated onion, apple, rice, salt, and pepper; add water and work in well. Place tomatoes, sliced onion, brown sugar, lemon juice, salt, and ginger in the bottom of a deep pot. Cut up heavy outside cabbage leaves and add to pot. Place about 2 tablespoons of meat mixture in center near the bottom of each cabbage leaf; fold bottom up, fold in each side, and roll up. Place in pot, open side down. Cover and simmer for 2 hours. Makes 8 servings.

Veal Roast with Sauerkraut

3-pound shoulder of veal, boned and tied
½ teaspoon salt
2 onions, sliced thin
1 clove garlic, minced
2 tablespoons olive oil
1 tablespoon paprika
1 pound sauerkraut, with juice

Season veal with salt and set aside. Sauté onions and garlic in olive oil in a Dutch oven until onions are golden; add paprika. Place veal roast in pot and surround with sauerkraut; add a little water if needed. Cover and simmer about 2 hours, or until tender. Slice and serve with sauerkraut gravy. Makes 6 to 8 servings.

Chicken Divan

2　10-ounce packages frozen broccoli stalks
1　cup water
¼　teaspoon salt
3　tablespoons butter
3　tablespoons flour
1½　cups milk
2　tablespoons grated Parmesan cheese
¼　teaspoon salt
⅛　teaspoon pepper
⅛　teaspoon nutmeg
4　thick slices cooked chicken

Preheat oven to 350°F. Place broccoli in a saucepan; add water and salt and cook for 10 minutes until tender. Drain. Meanwhile, melt butter in a saucepan; stir in flour, and when the mixture bubbles, add milk. Bring sauce to a boil, stirring constantly. Remove from heat and add cheese, salt, pepper, and nutmeg, stirring well. Place drained broccoli stalks in a buttered baking dish; top with chicken slices and cover with sauce. Bake 20 minutes. Makes 4 servings.

Upside-down Pineapple Muffins

¼ cup brown sugar
1½ cups flour
2½ teaspoons baking powder
1 teaspoon salt
½ cup sugar
1½ cups whole-bran cereal
1 8-ounce can crushed pineapple, with juice
¼ cup milk
1 egg
½ cup shortening

Preheat oven to 400°F. Generously butter muffin-pan cups; sprinkle about 1 teaspoon brown sugar into each cup and set aside. Sift together flour, baking powder, salt and sugar; set aside. Combine bran cereal, pineapple and juice, and milk in a mixing bowl. Let stand about 2 minutes, or until most of moisture is absorbed; add egg and shortening and mix well. Add sifted dry ingredients, stirring only until all ingredients are moistened. Fill muffin-pan cups ¾ full. Bake for 25 minutes, or until muffins are brown. Let stand in pan about 5 minutes; loosen muffins from sides of pan and invert on wire rack. Serve warm. Makes 1 dozen muffins.

Pumpkin Muffins

1½ cups sifted flour
2½ teaspoons baking powder
1 teaspoon salt
1 teaspoon cinnamon
½ teaspoon nutmeg
1¼ cups whole-bran cereal
⅔ cup milk
¾ cup seedless raisins
1 cup canned pumpkin
½ cup sugar
1 egg
½ cup soft shortening
1½ teaspoons sugar

Preheat oven to 400°F. Sift together flour, baking powder, salt, cinnamon, and nutmeg; set aside. Combine bran cereal, milk, raisins, pumpkin, and ½ cup sugar in a mixing bowl. Let stand 2 minutes to soften bran. Add egg and shortening; beat well. Add sifted ingredients, stirring only until all ingredients are moistened. Fill greased muffin-pan cups ¾ full; sprinkle 1½ teaspoons sugar over batter. Bake 35 minutes, or until muffins are golden brown. Serve hot. Makes 1 dozen muffins.

Bran Muffins

1½ cups whole-bran cereal
1 cup milk
1 egg
⅓ cup shortening
1½ cups flour
½ cup sugar
1 tablespoon baking powder
1 teaspoon salt

Preheat oven to 400°F. Stir together bran cereal and milk; let stand about 2 minutes until most of the moisture is absorbed. Add egg and shortening and beat well. Sift together flour, sugar, baking powder, and salt; add to batter, stirring only until all ingredients are moistened. Fill greased muffin-pan cups ¾ full. Bake 25 minutes, or until muffins are lightly browned. Serve hot. Makes 1 dozen muffins.

Bran Molasses Muffins

2 eggs
2 tablespoons molasses
1 cup milk
2 tablespoons melted butter
1 cup flour
1 cup bran flour
1 teaspoon baking powder
1 teaspoon baking soda
½ teaspoon salt

Preheat oven to 400°F. Beat eggs until lemon-colored; stir in molasses. Mix milk and melted butter. Sift together flours, baking powder, baking soda, and salt. Add dry ingredients to beaten eggs alternately with milk mixture, beginning and ending with dry mixture. Spoon into greased muffin pans. Bake 20 minutes, or until lightly browned. Makes 1 dozen muffins.

Oatmeal Muffins

1 cup raw oatmeal
½ cup brown sugar
1 cup buttermilk
1 egg, beaten
¼ cup salad oil
1 cup sifted flour
2 teaspoons baking powder
½ teaspoon baking soda
½ teaspoon salt
¼ teaspoon cinnamon

Preheat oven to 375°F. Combine oatmeal and brown sugar; add buttermilk and stir well. Stir together egg and salad oil; add to oatmeal mixture. Sift together flour, baking powder, baking soda, salt, and cinnamon; stir into oatmeal mixture, just until all ingredients are moistened. Spoon mixture into a greased and floured muffin tin, filling ⅔ full. Bake for 25 minutes, or until lightly browned. Makes 1 dozen muffins.

Apricot Bran Bread

1 cup finely cut dried apricots
1½ cups boiling water
¾ cup sugar
1½ cups whole-bran cereal
1 cup milk
2 eggs, slightly beaten
⅓ cup salad oil
1½ cups sifted flour
1 tablespoon baking powder
1 teaspoon salt
1 tablespoon sugar

Preheat oven to 350°F. Cover apricots with boiling water; let stand 10 minutes and drain well. Mix apricots and ¾ cup sugar; set aside. Combine bran cereal and milk in a large bowl; let stand a minute or two until most of the liquid is absorbed. Add eggs and oil and beat well. Sift together flour, baking powder, and salt; add to cereal mixture, stirring only until all ingredients are moistened. Fold in apricot mixture. Spread batter evenly in a well-greased wax-paper-lined 9×5-inch loaf pan. Sprinkle top with 1 tablespoon sugar. Bake for 1 hour, or until wooden pick inserted near center comes out clean. Let stand until thoroughly cooled before slicing. Makes 1 loaf.

Buttermilk Bran Bread

1⅔ cups crushed whole-bran cereal
4⅓ cups sifted flour
1 tablespoon baking soda
1 teaspoon sugar
1 teaspoon salt
2½ cups buttermilk

Preheat oven to 350°F. Mix together bran, flour, baking soda, sugar, and salt. Make a well in the center and pour in buttermilk. Work quickly and knead dough lightly; shape into a loaf and press into a greased 9 × 5-inch loaf pan. Bake 1 hour, or until firm and lightly browned. Makes 1 loaf.

Molasses Brown Bread

1 cup whole-bran cereal
½ cup seedless raisins
2 tablespoons shortening
⅓ cup molasses
¾ cup boiling water
1 egg
1 cup sifted flour
1 teaspoon baking soda
½ teaspoon salt
½ teaspoon cinnamon

Preheat oven to 350°F. Combine bran cereal, raisins, shortening, and molasses; add boiling water, stirring until shortening is melted. Add egg and beat well. Sift together flour, baking soda, salt, and cinnamon; add to bran mixture, stirring only until all ingredients are moistened. Pour batter into 2 well-greased cans, 4¼ inches deep and 3 inches in diameter, or a well-greased 9 × 5-inch loaf pan. Bake 45 minutes for the canned breads or about 35 minutes for the loaf, or until browned. Remove from cans or pan and slice. Serve hot. Makes 2 round small loaves, or 1 large loaf.

Whole-Wheat Griddle Cakes

2 eggs, separated
2 tablespoons salad oil
1½ cups milk
2 cups stale whole-wheat bread crumbs
½ cup flour
1 tablespoon baking powder
1 tablespoon sugar
½ teaspoon salt

Beat egg whites until stiff peaks form; set aside. Beat egg yolks and salad oil, add milk, and stir in bread crumbs. Sift together flour, baking powder, sugar, and salt; stir into egg yolk mixture. Fold into egg whites. Pour onto a lightly greased hot griddle, making 4-inch pancakes; brown on one side and then turn to brown on the other. Serve with syrup or jam, if desired. Makes 1 dozen pancakes.

Frosted Raisin Bars

1 cup flour
½ teaspoon baking powder
½ teaspoon salt
½ cup butter, softened
1 cup brown sugar
2 eggs
1 teaspoon vanilla
1 cup whole-bran cereal
1 cup seedless raisins

Preheat oven to 350°F. Sift together flour, baking powder, and salt; set aside. Cream butter and sugar until fluffy; add eggs and vanilla and beat well. Stir in bran cereal and raisins. Add sifted dry ingredients; mix well. Spread evenly in a greased 9-inch baking pan and bake 35 minutes, or until done. Cool. Frost with Sugar Icing. Makes 1½ dozen bars

SUGAR ICING:

1 cup sifted confectioners' sugar
1 tablespoon butter, softened
2 tablespoons milk
½ teaspoon vanilla

Beat all ingredients together until smooth and creamy. Spread evenly over bars.

Oatmeal Cookies

1 cup butter
1 cup sugar
2 eggs, beaten
2 cups oatmeal
2 cups flour
1 teaspoon baking powder
½ teaspoon baking soda
¼ teaspoon salt
1 teaspoon cinnamon
¼ cup milk
1 cup seedless raisins

Preheat oven to 350° F. Beat butter until fluffy and gradually add sugar; beat well and add eggs. Combine oatmeal, flour, baking powder, baking soda, salt, and cinnamon. Gradually add dry ingredients to batter, alternating with milk. Stir in raisins. Drop by tablespoonfuls onto a greased cookie sheet, about 1 inch apart. Bake 15 to 20 minutes, or until lightly browned. Makes about 3 dozen.

Chocolate Chip Bran Cookies

2 cups flour
½ teaspoon baking soda
½ teaspoon salt
1 cup soft butter
1½ cups sugar
2 eggs
1 teaspoon vanilla
1 cup whole-bran cereal
1 cup semisweet chocolate morsels

Preheat oven to 375°F. Sift together flour, baking soda, and salt; set aside. Cream butter and sugar until fluffy, add eggs and vanilla, and stir in bran cereal and chocolate morsels. Stir in sifted dry ingredients and mix well. Drop by level tablespoonfuls onto ungreased baking sheets and bake for 12 minutes, or until lightly browned. Makes about 5½ dozen cookies.

10

The Low-Fat Diet

A Low-Fat Diet is prescribed when the patient can't tolerate a high amount of emulsified fat or eat any foods that are gas-forming. Gallbladder sufferers are typical candidates for this kind of regime.

While a large variety of foods is allowed, it's important to eat only lean and well-trimmed meats and skim milk and skim milk products, and to limit your diet to only three eggs a week. No fried foods are allowed, and fats in the diet should be limited to the amounts in the listing.

Think of fat as your enemy; this will help you avoid foods that contain a lot of it. That includes all pork products, and roast duckling or other fatty poultry. Turn a skeptical eye on salad dressings that are made with eggs and oils, and use only crackers and breads that have been prepared with a minimum of shortening.

Good menu planning can produce a nutritionally adequate diet, and extra vitamins shouldn't be necessary to maintain good health.

	FOODS ALLOWED	FOODS TO OMIT
Beverages:	Skim milk or skim milk buttermilk—include at least 2 cups daily. Tea, coffee.	Whole milk, whole milk products, alcohol.
Eggs:	All kinds except fried —limit to three eggs per week. As many egg whites as desired.	Fried eggs.
Fats:	Limit to 1½ teaspoons a day, butter, margarine, or oil.	All fats, oils, salad dressings, or cream other than 1½ teaspoons allowed daily.
Cheese:	Uncreamed skim milk cottage cheese.	All others.
Breads and cereals:	Whole-grain or enriched bread and cereals, saltines, soda crackers, graham crackers—include 3 to 4 servings daily.	Crackers containing butter or fat, doughnuts, griddle cakes, waffles, breads and rolls made with butter or other fat, pastries and sweet rolls.
Vegetables:	All fresh, canned, or frozen except for those omitted—include 3 to 4 servings daily, at least 1 green and 1 yellow.	Broccoli, brussels sprouts, cabbage, cauliflower, turnips, cucumber, radishes, dried beans and peas.

Fruits:	All fruits except avocado. Include 1 to 2 servings of fruit daily, including 1 serving citrus fruit or juice.	Avocado.
Potato and substitutes:	White or sweet potato, rice, macaroni, spaghetti, plain noodles—include 1 potato daily.	Egg noodles, potato chips, fried potatoes, roasted potato.
Soup:	Broth, clear soups, vegetable soups with all fat removed. Cream soups made with skim milk and allowed amount of fat.	Cream soups made with whole milk or cream.
Meat, fish, and poultry:	Lean beef, veal, lamb, liver, chicken, turkey, cod, bass, pike, whitefish, flounder, haddock, halibut, perch, clams, oysters, shrimp, lobster, salmon and tuna packed without oil—include only 5 ounces of these daily. Include liver once a week.	Pork, ham, bacon, sausage, sardines, fish canned in oil, duck, goose, spiced meats and luncheon meats.

Desserts:	Fruit-flavored gelatin, fruit whips made with egg whites, puddings made with skim milk, angel food cake, ices, sherbets made with skim milk.	Ice cream, puddings, and sherbets made with whole milk and egg yolks; commercial puddings, pastry, pie; desserts containing chocolate, nuts, cream, butter, margarine, and coconut.
Miscellaneous:	Cocoa powder, dressing made from tomato juice, all mild herbs, salt, pepper, garlic.	Fried and spicy foods, gravy, salad dressings, chocolate, olives, peanut butter, nuts, coconut.

SUGGESTED MENU PLAN

Breakfast
Fruit juice
Cereal with skim milk
Bread
*½ teaspoon butter
Jelly
Beverage

Lunch
Lean meat, fish, poultry, or egg
Potato or substitute
Vegetable
Fruit
Bread
*½ teaspoon butter
Jelly
1 cup skim milk

Dinner
Lean meat, fish, or poultry, or egg
Potato or substitute
Vegetable
Salad
Dessert or fruit
*½ teaspoon butter in vegetable
1 cup skim milk
Beverage

*This diet is restricted to 40 grams of fat. To reduce fat to 25 grams, omit butter or substitutes and eggs.

RECIPES

In addition to these recipes for a Low-Fat Diet, the following recipes may also be used:

Beverages:
Slim Skimnog 54

Eggs:
Baked Egg Florentine 32
Grape Soufflé 74
Hard-Cooked Eggs 30
Poached Eggs 31
Soft-Cooked Eggs 30
Spinach Soufflé 38

Vegetables:
Boiled Beets 36
Green Beans Oregano 119
Harvard Beets #2 230
Spinach Cottage Cheese Bake (use allowed cottage cheese) 38
Zucchini 214

Potato and substitutes:
Herb Rice (omit butter) 78
Rice-Stuffed Peaches (omit butter) 78
Rice with Spicy Tomato Sauce 235

Fruits:
Applesauce 104
Broiled Bananas 78
Poached Pears 105

Soup:
Beef Bouillon 33
Chicken Broth 33
Cold Borscht 209
Potato Soup (use skim milk) 162

Meat:
Apple Muffin Burgers 101
Baked Beef Stew 42
Filet Mignon Roast 120
Fluffy Meat Loaf (use allowed bread) 41
Meat Loaf 144
Meat Loaf with Peach Sauce 121
Potted Lamb Stew 102
Veal Balls in Apricot Sauce 101
Veal Stew 79

Poultry:
>Baked Chicken and Apricots (omit butter) 103
Baked Chicken Stew 125
Baked Orange Chicken 43
Chicken on Rice 238
Chicken Livers Oregano 81
Chopped Liver and Bean Spread 82
Orange Glazed Chicken 218
Peachy Baked Chicken (use skim milk) 217
Poached Breast of Chicken 102

Fish:
>Boiled Fish 104
Broiled Lemon Flounder 43
Poached Haddock 126

Desserts:
>Angel Food Cake 66
Banana Gelatin Cup 83
Chocolate Chiffon Pudding (use skim milk) 47
Gelatin Parfait 106
Lemon Ice 22
Orange Sponge Cake 85
Peachy Gelatin 45
Prune Whip 105

Tomato Clam Soup

1½ cups tomato juice
½ cup clam juice
½ teaspoon lemon juice
⅛ teaspoon pepper

Combine tomato juice, clam juice, lemon juice, and pepper. Heat through. Makes 2 servings.

Cream of Tomato Soup

2 cups tomato juice
2 cups skim milk buttermilk
1 tablespoon lemon juice
1 teaspoon sugar
½ teaspoon salt

Combine tomato juice, buttermilk, lemon juice, sugar, and salt in a jar and shake well. Serve hot or cold. Makes 4 servings.

Oriental Spinach Soup

1 10-ounce package frozen whole-leaf spinach
2 10½-ounce cans condensed chicken broth
1 soup can water
1 tablespoon cornstarch
½ cup diced celery
2 tablespoons sliced green onion
2 teaspoons soy sauce

Cook spinach as directed on package; drain. Combine chicken broth and water in a saucepan; stir in cornstarch, celery, green onion, and soy sauce. Bring to a boil; simmer 5 minutes. Add cooked spinach and serve hot. Makes 8 servings.

Carrots with Pineapple

1 16-ounce can tiny whole carrots
1 8¾-ounce can pineapple tidbits, with juice
1 tablespoon brown sugar

Drain carrots and place in a small saucepan. Add pineapple tidbits with juice and sugar; stir and heat together. Makes 4 servings.

Green Beans and Tomatoes

1 16-ounce can green beans, with liquid
1 cup canned peeled tomatoes, with liquid
1 tablespoon chopped onion
½ teaspoon brown sugar
½ teaspoon oregano
1 teaspoon lemon juice

Drain bean and tomato juice into a saucepan. Add onion, sugar, oregano, and lemon juice; heat and stir until well blended. Add beans and tomatoes. Serve hot. Makes 4 servings.

Acorn Squash with Applesauce Filling

2 acorn squashes
1 cup applesauce
2 teaspoons brown sugar
2 tablespoons seedless raisins

Preheat oven to 400°F. Scrub, halve, and remove seeds from squashes. Mix together applesauce, brown sugar, and raisins; fill cavities of squash halves. Place in a flat baking dish, adding water to cover 1 inch of squash. Cover and bake 20 minutes. Remove cover and bake 15 minutes longer, or until tender. Makes 4 servings.

Yogurt Creamed Spinach

1 10-ounce package frozen chopped spinach
½ teaspoon salt
½ teaspoon onion salt
¼ teaspoon nutmeg
¼ cup skim milk yogurt

Place spinach in a saucepan and add 1 inch of water. Add salt, onion salt, and nutmeg and cook until tender. Drain. Stir in yogurt. Makes 4 servings.

Oil-Free Dressing

2 ounces wine vinegar
4 ounces water
½ teaspoon sugar
¼ teaspoon salt
Dash pepper
Dash celery salt

Combine all ingredients; mix vigorously and pour over salad. Makes ¾ cup dressing.

Tomato Juice Dressing

1 cup tomato juice
¼ cup lemon juice
2 tablespoons finely grated celery
1 clove garlic, minced
1 teaspoon sugar
½ teaspoon salt
Dash pepper

Combine all ingredients in a jar. Shake vigorously and refrigerate several hours before using. Makes 1⅓ cups dressing for salads.

Spaghetti with Tomato Sauce

1 8-ounce package spaghetti
1 teaspoon salt
2 quarts boiling water
2 8-ounce cans tomato sauce
2 tablespoons tomato paste
½ cup finely sliced celery
¼ cup finely diced green pepper
½ teaspoon oregano

Cook spaghetti in salted boiling water; drain. Meanwhile, empty tomato sauce into a saucepan. Add tomato paste, celery, green pepper, and oregano; mix well. Cover and simmer 10 minutes, or until vegetables are soft. Pour over drained spaghetti and serve. Makes 4 servings.

Flank Steak Teriyaki

1 flank steak, about 2 pounds
¼ cup soy sauce
1 tablespoon brown sugar
½ teaspoon ginger
1 clove crushed garlic

Place flank steak on a broiling rack. Combine soy sauce, sugar, ginger, and garlic. Brush half the mixture on top of steak; broil in a preheated broiler for 10 minutes. Turn and brush remaining sauce on top of steak; broil 5 to 10 minutes more, depending on desired degree of rareness. Slice steak on a wide angle, as for London Broil. Makes 4 servings.

Swiss Steak

2-pound slice of top round steak
2 tablespoons flour
½ teaspoon salt
¼ teaspoon pepper
1 cup grapefruit juice
2 teaspoons brown sugar

Trim steak of all excess fat. Combine flour, salt, and pepper; pound into surface of steak on all sides. Sprinkle a skillet with additional salt and sear meat on all sides. Combine grapefruit juice and brown sugar; pour around steak. Cover and cook 1 hour, or until tender. Makes 6 servings.

Potted Veal Roast

2-pound boned rolled shoulder of veal roast
1 onion, sliced thin
1 clove garlic, minced
½ teaspoon salt
½ teaspoon pepper
1 teaspoon brown sugar
2 teaspoons paprika
1 can beef bouillon
2 carrots, scraped and grated

In a Dutch oven, arrange veal and onion. Add garlic, salt, pepper, brown sugar, and paprika. Pour bouillon around roast and add grated carrots; cover and simmer 2 hours, or until tender. Serve sliced with gravy. Makes 6 servings.

Veal and Peppers

2 16-ounce cans stewed tomatoes
2 tablespoons tomato paste
1 onion, sliced
2 green peppers, seeded and cubed
2 pounds veal, cubed
½ teaspoon salt
¼ teaspoon pepper
¼ teaspoon rosemary

Preheat oven to 350°F. Empty stewed tomatoes into a Dutch oven or similar covered casserole; add tomato paste and stir. Add onion, green peppers, veal, salt, pepper, and rosemary; mix well. Cover tightly and bake 1 hour, or until veal is tender. Makes 6 to 8 servings.

Veal Scallopine in Tomato Sauce

1 pound veal scallopine slices
2 cups tomato juice
1 teaspoon cornstarch
1 teaspoon oregano
½ teaspoon garlic salt
½ teaspoon salt

Flatten veal slices and place in a large skillet. Stir together remaining ingredients; pour over veal. Cover and simmer 25 minutes. Makes 4 servings.

Lamb Shanks L'Orange

8 lamb shanks
Meat tenderizer
1 6-ounce can undiluted frozen orange juice
1 tablespoon parsley
1 teaspoon brown sugar
½ teaspoon salt

Preheat oven to 325°F. Sprinkle lamb shanks with meat tenderizer according to label directions. In a small saucepan, heat and stir orange juice concentrate, parsley, brown sugar, and salt. Heat and stir until juice is melted. Arrange shanks in a roasting pan and brush with sauce. Roast 1 hour, basting occasionally with remaining sauce; reheat remaining sauce and pour over lamb shanks when ready to serve. Makes 8 servings.

Leg of Lamb Café

1 half a leg of lamb, shank side
½ teaspoon salt
½ teaspoon paprika
¼ teaspoon garlic salt
2 teaspoons instant decaffeinated coffee
1 cup boiling water

Preheat oven to 400°F. Season lamb with salt, paprika, and garlic salt. Roast for 30 minutes. Stir instant coffee into boiling water; pour over roast. Continue roasting 30 to 45 minutes longer, until done to your liking. Makes 6 servings.

Shish Kebab

2 pounds lean lamb cubes
2 green peppers, seeded and cubed
24 medium mushroom caps
12 small white peeled onions
½ teaspoon salt
¼ teaspoon garlic salt
⅛ teaspoon pepper

Skewer alternately chunks of lamb, green pepper, mushrooms, and onions. Season with salt, garlic salt, and pepper. Place on a pan and broil in a preheated broiler 15 minutes, turning once. Makes 6 servings.

Chicken Luau

6 boneless chicken breasts
½ teaspoon salt
1 13½-ounce can pineapple chunks, with juice
1 tablespoon cornstarch
1 teaspoon brown sugar
¼ teaspoon ground ginger

Preheat oven to 350°F. Arrange chicken breasts in a small baking dish and sprinkle with salt. In a small bowl, drain pineapple juice into cornstarch and blend until smooth. Add pineapple chunks, brown sugar, and ginger and pour over chicken breasts, coating them well. Bake for 25 minutes, basting occasionally with sauce in the pan. Makes 6 servings.

Potted Chicken with Artichoke Hearts

3-pound broiler chicken, cut up
1 can whole tomatoes
1 onion, sliced
1 green pepper, cut up
1 can artichoke hearts, with liquid
1 tablespoon lemon juice
1 teaspoon sugar
½ teaspoon salt
2 teaspoons paprika

Place cleaned chicken in a heavy skillet. Add tomatoes, onion, green pepper, and artichoke hearts and liquid. Add lemon juice, sugar, and salt; mix well. Sprinkle paprika over chicken. Cover tightly and simmer 45 minutes, or until tender. Makes 4 servings.

Chicken Mandarin

1 broiler chicken, quartered
½ teaspoon salt
1 tablespoon cornstarch
⅛ teaspoon marjoram
⅛ teaspoon rosemary
1 8-ounce can mandarin oranges, with juice

Sprinkle chicken with salt; arrange in a broiling pan and broil in a preheated broiler 20 minutes, turning to cook both sides. Meanwhile, combine cornstarch, marjoram, rosemary, and mandarin orange juice in a saucepan; mix until smooth. Cook and stir until sauce is thick. Add orange slices, pour over broiled chicken, and serve. Makes 4 servings.

Cucumber Cream Broiled Fillets

1 pound fillet of flounder, 4 slices
¼ cup skim milk yogurt
1 teaspoon lemon juice
½ teaspoon salt
½ teaspoon sugar
½ teaspoon paprika
¼ teaspoon Worchestershire sauce
½ medium cucumber, peeled

Arrange fillets in a flat baking pan. In a blender, combine yogurt, lemon juice, salt, sugar, paprika, and Worcestershire sauce; blend until smooth. Slice 8 thin slices of cucumber and reserve for garnish; cut up remaining cucumber and add to other ingredients in the blender. Blend until smooth and spread mixture on fish. Broil in a preheated broiler 15 minutes, or until fish flakes easily. Garnish with cucumber slices and serve. Makes 4 servings.

Poached Salmon

2-pound slice center-cut fresh salmon
1 quart water
½ cup cider vinegar
1 onion, sliced
3 whole cloves
2 sprigs fresh dill
1 bay leaf
1 teaspoon sugar
1 teaspoon salt

Place salmon and remaining ingredients in a large saucepan. Bring to a boil, then reduce heat and simmer 15 to 20 minutes, or until salmon is flaky but still whole. Remove from water and serve hot or chilled. Makes 6 servings.

Zuppa de Clams on Linguine

2 dozen fresh clams
2 cups tomato juice
1 cup bottled clam juice
½ teaspoon oregano
¼ teaspoon thyme
¼ teaspoon salt
¼ teaspoon garlic salt
8 ounces cooked linguine

Wash clams just before cooking. Combine tomato juice, clam juice, oregano, thyme, salt, and garlic salt in a large saucepan; stir well. Add clams in the shell. Cover and cook 5 to 8 minutes, until all shells have opened. Serve in soup plates on cooked linguine, leaving clams in the shells. Makes 4 servings.

Poached Shrimp

20 large shrimp, peeled and cleaned
2 cups chicken broth
1 bay leaf
1 tablespoon minced parsley
½ teaspoon sugar
½ teaspoon salt
1 tablespoon lemon juice

Cut shrimp partially through lengthwise, flatten, and place in a single layer in a large skillet. Add chicken broth, bay leaf, parsley, sugar, salt, and lemon juice. Bring to a boil, then simmer 5 minutes, stirring occasionally. Serve at once. Makes 4 servings.

Broiled Shrimp

1 pound large shrimp
½ cup lemon juice
½ teaspoon garlic salt
¼ teaspoon paprika
1 tablespoon chopped parsley

Peel and clean shrimp, leaving tails on. Split down the center and press flat to achieve butterfly shape. Place shrimp in a flat baking dish; mix together lemon juice, garlic salt, paprika, and chopped parsley and pour over shrimp. Refrigerate 1 hour in this marinade, turning frequently. Place under preheated broiler for 3 minutes on each side. Serve at once. Makes 4 servings.

Fruit Compote

1 16-ounce can peeled apricot halves, with juice
1 16-ounce can peach halves, with juice
½ cup orange juice
Juice and rind of ½ lemon
2 teaspoons honey

Drain apricot and peach juice into a saucepan; add orange juice, lemon juice and rind, and honey. Heat thoroughly, reducing liquid to desired thickness. Pour over fruit and chill. Makes 6 servings.

Mapled Pears

1 16-ounce can pear halves, drained
½ cup maple-flavored syrup
¼ teaspoon nutmeg
2 tablespoons white raisins

Combine pears, maple syrup, nutmeg, and raisins in a small saucepan. Simmer for 5 minutes. Cool and chill. Makes 4 servings.

Pineapple-Grape Sherbet

1 6-ounce can frozen pineapple juice concentrate
1 6-ounce can frozen grape juice concentrate
3½ cups cold water
1 cup nonfat dry milk
2 tablespoons sugar

Empty juice concentrates into a mixing bowl; add water, dry milk, and sugar. Beat until well blended. Pour into two ice cube trays and freeze until half frozen, 1 to 2 hours. Empty into a large chilled mixing bowl and beat on low speed until mixture is softened, then beat on high speed 3 to 5 minutes, until mixture is creamy but not liquid. Pour into freezer containers or ice cube trays and freeze until firm. Makes 10 servings.

Apricot Fluff

1 5-ounce jar strained apricots for babies
1 tablespoon sugar
1 teaspoon vanilla
1 teaspoon lemon juice
1 teaspoon grated lemon rind
1 teaspoon unflavored gelatin
1 tablespoon cold water
2 egg whites

Stir together strained apricots, sugar, vanilla, and lemon juice and rind. Soften gelatin in cold water, then dissolve over hot water in a double boiler. Beat egg whites until frothy; add gelatin and beat until very stiff. Fold into apricot mixture and spoon into sherbet glasses. Chill. Makes 4 servings.

Coffee Custard

2 tablespoons instant coffee
¼ teaspoon salt
⅓ cup flour
2 cups skim milk, scalded
¼ cup sugar
2 eggs, slightly beaten
1 teaspoon vanilla

Combine coffee, salt, and flour in the top of a double boiler; add scalded milk slowly to make a smooth sauce. Add sugar, eggs, and vanilla. Cook over hot water, stirring constantly, until thick. Pour into dessert dishes and chill. Makes 5 servings.

11

The Low-Sodium Diet

Normally, when your doctor orders a sodium-restricted diet, you must cut out all use of salt and avoid using foods with a high natural sodium content, and also products with the word "sodium" listed in their ingredients. That should reduce your normal intake of sodium to about half the normal amount, or 2,500 mg. of sodium daily.

If your doctor advises an even lower level of sodium, and specifies how many milligrams of sodium you'll be permitted each day, you'll have to eliminate other sources of sodium, things we usually don't think of in terms of being "salty." On an extreme low-sodium diet, you may have to check the sodium levels in the water with your water company to find out how many milligrams of sodium there are in each gallon of water, considering the different chemicals added in each area to make water fit for local consumption. You may also have to eliminate milk from your diet or substitute low-sodium milk.

Luckily, herbs and spices may be used freely on a low-sodium diet, and better cooking can often result. This diet allows a large variety of foods and is nutritionally adequate, but some potassium loss can occur if your doctor has also prescribed a diuretic. Potassium loss can generally be avoided by serving a daily glass of orange juice and including bananas and other potassium-rich foods in the diet.

	FOODS ALLOWED	FOODS TO OMIT
Beverages:	Milk—limit to 2½ cups daily. Cocoa, coffee, tea, low-sodium carbonated beverages—limit to 1 cup daily.	Cultured buttermilk, instant cocoa mixes, prepared beverage mixes, regular carbonated drinks, chemically softened water.
Eggs:	All kinds—limit to 1 daily.	None.
Fats:	Unsalted butter, unsalted margarine, vegetable shortening, oil, lard, chicken fat, unsalted salad dressings, cream—limit to 3 ounces daily.	Salted butter or margarine, commercial mayonnaise and salad dressings, bacon fat.
Cheese:	Unsalted cottage cheese, unsalted special cheeses.	All others.
Breads and cereals:	Low-sodium bread and rolls, unsalted matzoh, bread products made with sodium-free baking powder and without baking soda or salt—include 2 to 4 slices daily. Regular cooked cereal without salt; puffed rice, puffed wheat, and any other dry cereal without sodium on the label.	All bakery products made with salt, baking powder, or baking soda; all prepared mixes. Self-rising flour, pretzels, all commercial crackers, all quick-cooking cereals containing disodium phosphate, and all other dry cereals.

Vegetables:	Low-sodium canned vegetables and vegetable juices, plain frozen vegetables without sodium on the label, all fresh vegetables except those on the nonallowed list.	All regular canned vegetables and vegetable juices, all frozen vegetables with prepared sauces, all frozen vegetables with sodium added. Artichokes, beets and beet greens, carrots, celery, Swiss chard, dandelion greens, hominy, kale, mustard greens, sauerkraut, spinach, and white turnips.
Fruit:	All—include at least 1 to 2 servings daily, and citrus fruit or juice once daily.	None.
Potato and substitutes:	White potato, sweet potato, rice, noodles, macaroni, spaghetti, all prepared without salt. Include 1 potato daily.	Potato chips; all pasta in prepared sauces that contain sodium.
Soup:	Unsalted broth and bouillon, unsalted cream soups made from allowed vegetables and milk.	Commercial soups in cans and packages; restaurant soup.

Meat, fish, and poultry:	Beef, veal, lamb, pork, chicken, and fresh fish prepared without salt—serve 6 ounces daily.	Brains, kidneys, salted or smoked meats, delicatessen meats, ham, luncheon meats, salt pork, sausage, salted or smoked fish, all shellfish, frozen fish, canned products, and bacon.
Desserts:	Desserts prepared without salt, baking powder, and baking soda, or without any sodium on the label. Plain gelatin desserts, low-sodium ice cream and sherbet.	Desserts prepared with salt, baking powder, baking soda; all commercial mixes, gelatin desserts, ice cream, and sherbet.
Miscellaneous:	Herbs and spices, vinegar in moderation, unsalted chocolate products, unsalted peanut butter, preserves without sodium benzoate, honey, syrup, sugar, gumdrops, hard candy, marshmallows, plain mints.	Salt, salted nuts, salted peanut butter; monosodium glutamate; olives, all commercial condiments, mayonnaise; meat tenderizer containing sodium, gravy containing sodium, bouillon cubes; prepared mustard, celery salt, onion salt, garlic salt, Worcestershire, soy, Tabasco, molasses.

SUGGESTED MENU PLAN

Breakfast
Fruit
Cereal with ½ cup milk
1 egg
Low-sodium bread
Unsalted butter
Beverage

Lunch
Meat, fish, or poultry
Potato or substitute
Vegetable
Fruit
Low-sodium bread
Unsalted butter
Beverage
Milk

Dinner
Meat, fish, or poultry
Potato or substitute
Vegetable
Salad
Dessert or fruit
Low-sodium bread
Unsalted butter
Milk

RECIPES

In addition to these recipes for a Low-Sodium Diet, the following recipes may be used:

Eggs:
>   Carrot Soufflé (omit salt) 55
>   Hard-Cooked Eggs 30
>   Poached Eggs (omit salt) 31
>   Soft-Cooked Eggs 30

Vegetables:
>   Broiled Tomatoes 214
>   Carrot Strips (omit salt) 74
>   Brussels Sprouts (omit salt) 139, 211
>   Green Beans in Tomato Sauce (omit salt) 39
>   Red Cabbage (omit salt) 213
>   Spinach in Orange-Butter Sauce (omit salt) 75
>   Squash Rings (omit salt) 75
>   Sweet and Sour Red Cabbage (omit salt) 142
>   Tender Peas (omit salt) 76
>   Zucchini 214

Potato and substitutes:
>   Baked Sweet Potatoes (omit salt) 40
>   Herb Rice (omit salt) 78
>   Orange Rice (omit salt) 40
>   Parsleyed Potatoes (omit salt) 215
>   Rice-Stuffed Peaches 78
>   Scalloped Potatoes (omit salt) 63
>   Wild Rice and Mushroom Ring (omit salt) 143

Fruit:
>   Baked Apple 44
>   Broiled Bananas 78

Soup:
>   Broccoli Milk Soup (omit salt) 208
>   Cold Borscht (omit salt) 209

Meat:
> Filet Mignon Roast (omit salt) 120
> Leg of Lamb Café (omit salt) 170
> Swiss Steak (omit salt) 168

Poultry:
> Apricot Jellied Turkey Roll 64
> Baked Chicken and Apricots (omit salt) 103
> Broiled Tarragon Chicken (omit salt) 82
> Chicken Livers Oregano (omit salt) 81
> Chicken Luau (omit salt) 171
> Chicken Mandarin (omit salt) 172
> Orange Glazed Chicken (omit salt) 218
> Peachy Baked Chicken (omit salt) 217

Fish:
> Halibut Mousse (omit salt) 125
> Poached Haddock (omit salt) 126
> Poached Salmon (omit salt) 173

Desserts:
> Apricot Fluff 177
> Baked Lemon Pudding (omit salt) 244
> Banana Freeze 44
> Banana-Lime Gelatin 45
> Banana Gelatin Cup 83
> Blancmange (omit salt) 240
> Caramel Pudding (omit salt) 241
> Coconut Pie Crust 249
> Coffee Custard 177
> Creamy Rice Pudding (omit salt) 46
> Fruit Compote 175
> Macaroons 248
> Mapled Pears 176
> Peachy Gelatin 45
> Pineapple-Grape Sherbet 176
> Snow Pudding (omit salt) 243
> Sugar Cookies 85
> Vanilla Cookies 48
> Vanilla Pudding (omit salt) 241

Shirred Eggs

6 eggs
2 tablespoons unsalted butter
2 tablespoons light cream
Dash white pepper

Preheat oven to 400°F. Break eggs one at a time into a buttered shallow baking dish, being careful not to break yolks. Melt butter, remove from heat, and stir in cream and pepper; drizzle over eggs. Bake about 20 minutes, or until eggs are set. Serve at once. Makes 6 servings.

Scrambled Eggs and Corn

2 ears cooked corn
2 tablespoons unsalted butter
4 eggs
Dash pepper
⅛ teaspoon dried tarragon

Cut corn from cobs. Melt butter in a large skillet; add corn. Beat eggs together and pour over corn. Sprinkle with pepper and tarragon. Cook over medium heat, stirring cooked portion toward the center of the skillet to permit liquid mixture to run toward the edge. Serve as soon as eggs are set. Makes 2 or 3 servings.

Cottage Cheese Chive Scramble

4 eggs
Dash white pepper
1 tablespoon chopped chives
1 tablespoon unsalted butter
½ cup low-sodium cottage cheese

Break eggs into a bowl and beat lightly; add pepper and chives. Heat butter in a large skillet. Pour in egg mixture and reduce heat just enough to cook eggs quickly, lifting mixture from the bottom and sides as it thickens to allow uncooked portion to flow to the bottom. When eggs are almost thickened throughout, stir cottage cheese into egg mixture. Remove from heat as soon as cheese is melted and eggs coated; serve at once. Makes 2 to 4 servings.

Tomato-Pepper Omelet

2 tablespoons unsalted butter
1 onion, diced
1 sweet green pepper, diced
1 tomato, diced
4 eggs
2 tablespoons milk

Melt butter in a skillet; add onion, green pepper, and tomato. Stir and cook several minutes, until onion is translucent. Beat eggs and milk together; pour over vegetables. Cook, pushing mixture to the middle of the skillet as it solidifies, letting liquid egg run to the edge. Fold and serve. Makes 2 to 3 servings.

Vegetable Soup

4 beef bones with marrow
2 quarts water
2 onions, sliced
½ cup barley
2 carrots, peeled and sliced
3 tomatoes, cut up
1 large potato, peeled and cut up
2 stalks celery, sliced
½ pound trimmed green beans, cut up
½ pound shelled peas
1 bay leaf
½ teaspoon sugar
¼ teaspoon pepper
2 tablespoons farina (optional)

Place beef bones in a large pot and cover with water; add sliced onions and barley. Bring to a boil, then reduce heat and simmer about 30 minutes, skimming residue off the surface occasionally. Add remaining ingredients except farina. Cover and cook 30 minutes, or until vegetables are tender. If thicker soup is desired, add farina and stir until cooked through. Makes 8 servings.

Mushroom-Barley Soup

2 beef marrow bones
½ pound sliced fresh mushrooms
⅓ cup barley
1 onion, diced
1 carrot, scraped and diced fine
1½ quarts water
2 sprigs dillweed, chopped fine
2 sprigs parsley, chopped fine
¼ teaspoon pepper
3 tablespoons farina
1 cup milk

Place bones, mushrooms, barley, onion, and carrot in a deep pot. Add water, dill, parsley, and pepper. Bring to a boil, then reduce heat and cover. Simmer 1 hour. Stir farina into milk; add to soup, stirring constantly, and let soup thicken. Makes 8 servings.

Broccoli with Parsley/Butter Sauce

2 10-ounce packages frozen broccoli
2 tablespoons unsalted butter
1 tablespoon lemon juice
1 tablespoon chopped parsley

Cook broccoli according to package directions; drain. Melt butter and stir in lemon juice and parsley. Pour over drained broccoli and serve at once. Makes 6 servings.

Salt-Free Spinach

1 10-ounce package frozen chopped spinach
1 tablespoon chopped onion
¼ teaspoon ground nutmeg
⅛ teaspoon white pepper
2 tablespoons unsalted butter

Place spinach in a saucepan with ½ inch of water in pan. Add onion, nutmeg, and pepper. Cook, covered, until tender; drain well and stir in butter until melted. Makes 4 servings.

Yellow Squash with Orange-Dill Sauce

2 pounds summer crookneck or yellow squash
¼ cup unsalted butter
2 tablespoons frozen orange juice concentrate, thawed
1 small onion, sliced thin
1 teaspoon sugar
1 teaspoon chopped dillweed

Wash squash; trim stem and blossom ends, but do not pare. Cut into ½-inch slices. Melt butter in a skillet; stir in orange juice concentrate. Add squash and onion and sprinkle with sugar and dill. Cook, covered, over moderate heat for 10 to 15 minutes, until squash is tender. Makes 4 to 6 servings.

Salt-Free French Dressing

⅔ cup salad oil
⅓ cup vinegar
¼ teaspoon dry mustard
¼ teaspoon paprika
⅛ teaspoon pepper

Combine all ingredients in a bottle and shake well. Store, covered, in refrigerator until ready to use. Shake well before using. Makes 1 cup dressing.

Salt-Free Meat Loaf

2 pounds lean ground beef
1 small onion, grated
1 egg
½ cup unseasoned bread crumbs
¼ cup chopped parsley
2 tablespoons grated Parmesan cheese
¼ teaspoon pepper
⅛ teaspoon cinnamon

Preheat oven to 350°F. Combine all ingredients, mixing well. Pack into a loaf pan and bake 1 hour. Makes 6 to 8 servings.

Herb Burgers

1 pound ground beef
¼ teaspoon pepper
1 tablespoon minced onion
¼ teaspoon marjoram
⅓ teaspoon thyme
1 tablespoon chopped parsley

Combine all ingredients, mixing well. Shape into patties and grill, broil, or fry. Makes 4 servings.

Surprise Burgers

1 **pound ground beef**
1 **tablespoon grated onion**
2 **tablespoons chopped parsley**
¼ **teaspoon pepper**
4 **thin slices tomato**
4 **thin slices onion**

Break up beef in a mixing bowl and work in grated onion, parsley, and pepper. Shape into 8 thin patties. Top 4 patties with a slice of tomato and a slice of onion; cover with remaining patties and press edges together to seal. Broil 3 to 4 minutes on each side, or to desired doneness. Makes 4 servings.

Brisket Pot Roast

4-pound brisket of beef, preferably a lean first cut
2 **onions, sliced**
1 **cup water**
2 **bay leaves**
¼ **teaspoon pepper**
¼ **teaspoon paprika**

Preheat oven to 325°F. Set beef in a Dutch oven or covered baking pan; cover with sliced onions and add water. Add bay leaves to water and sprinkle beef with pepper and paprika. Cover and roast about 3 hours, or until tender. Makes 6 to 8 servings.

Beef Stew au Vin

2   pounds lean cubed beef
3   large tomatoes, cut in small wedges
4   carrots, cut in 1-inch lengths
4   stalks celery, cut in 1-inch lengths
2   onions, sliced thin
2   sweet peppers, seeded and cut up
6   potatoes, pared and cut up
½   cup Burgundy wine
½   cup water
2   bay leaves
¼   teaspoon pepper
¼   teaspoon dried basil

Preheat oven to 350°F. Combine all ingredients in a Dutch oven or other large, tight-lidded pan. Cover and bake 1½ hours, or until meat is fork-tender. Makes 6 to 8 servings.

London Broil

2-pound flank steak
½   small onion, diced fine
½   clove garlic, minced
¼   teaspoon black pepper
2   tablespoons salad oil

Arrange flank steak flat on a broiling pan. Combine onion, garlic, pepper, and oil; rub over both sides of steak. Marinate ½ hour at room temperature. Broil in preheated broiler about 5 minutes on each side. Carve into thin slices on an extreme diagonal across the grain. Makes 4 to 6 servings.

Veal Balls in Citrus Sauce

1½ pounds ground veal
1 cup oatmeal
2 eggs
1 tablespoon brown sugar
⅛ teaspoon ground cloves
⅛ teaspoon nutmeg

Combine all ingredients; shape into 1-inch balls and chill.
Brown lightly in hot salad oil. Drain off excess oil. Pour Citrus
Sauce over veal balls and cook about 45 minutes over low heat.
Gently stir in orange pieces; heat until warm and serve at once.
Makes 6 to 8 servings.

CITRUS SAUCE:

½ cup brown sugar
4 teaspoons cornstarch
2 teaspoons grated orange peel
1 cup orange juice
1 cup water
¼ cup lemon juice
1 orange, peeled, cut into bite-sized pieces

Combine sugar and cornstarch; blend in orange peel and orange
juice, stirring until smooth. Add water and lemon juice; reserve
orange pieces. Proceed as above.

Veal Marsala

1 pound thinly sliced veal
¼ cup flour
2 tablespoons olive oil
1 tablespoon unsalted butter or margarine
½ cup Marsala wine
1 tablespoon chopped parsley

Dredge veal slices in flour. Heat olive oil and butter in a heavy skillet; lightly brown veal slices, turning to brown both sides. Reduce heat; pour Marsala wine over veal and sprinkle with chopped parsley. Cover and simmer 10 minutes, or until tender. Serve at once. Makes 4 servings.

Veal Paprikash

2 pounds thinly sliced veal
2 tablespoons sweet paprika
⅛ teaspoon pepper
3 tablespoons unsalted butter or margarine
3 tomatoes
½ cup water
¾ cup light cream

Sprinkle veal with paprika and pepper. Heat butter in a heavy skillet; brown veal on both sides. Cut up tomatoes and put in a blender with ½ cup water; puree and pour over veal. Cover and simmer 35 minutes, or until tender. Just before serving, add cream; heat through but do not bring to a boil. Serve at once. Makes 6 servings.

Broiled Lamb with Herb Marinade

6 large shoulder lamb chops
½ cup Burgundy wine
¼ cup salad oil
½ teaspoon pepper
1½ tablespoons chopped parsley
1 clove garlic
1 small bay leaf
¼ teaspoon dried thyme
¼ teaspoon dried rosemary

Place lamb chops in a baking dish. Combine all other ingredients; pour over the lamb chops and cover. Refrigerate several hours or overnight, turning chops occasionally. Remove chops from marinade when ready to cook; broil in a preheated broiler 5 minutes on each side. Baste occasionally with remaining marinade. Makes 6 servings.

Barbecued Ribs of Lamb

3 pounds lamb riblets
½ cup apricot jam
2 tablespoons prepared mustard
1 teaspoon crushed rosemary
½ clove crushed garlic

Preheat oven to 325°F. Place riblets on a rack in a shallow roasting pan; bake about 1½ hours. Drain off all drippings. Combine apricot jam, mustard, rosemary, and garlic; brush mixture over ribs and bake 30 minutes longer, turning ribs and basting with additional sauce. Makes 6 servings.

Baked Chicken with Herbs

2 broiler chickens, quartered
⅛ teaspoon pepper
½ cup unsalted butter or margarine, softened
1 clove garlic, crushed
1 cup fine dry bread crumbs
¼ cup chopped parsley
1 teaspoon rosemary
½ teaspoon dry mustard

Preheat oven to 375°F. Sprinkle chicken lightly with pepper. Combine butter and garlic. On a piece of wax paper, combine bread crumbs, parsley, rosemary, and dry mustard. Spread chicken quarters on both sides with butter-garlic mixture; dip in bread crumb mixture to coat well. Place on foil-lined baking pan and bake 1 hour, or until chicken is tender. Makes 8 servings.

Lemonade Broiled Chicken

1 broiler chicken, quartered
2 cups lemonade
¼ teaspoon rosemary
¼ teaspoon paprika

Marinate chicken parts in lemonade for 1 hour. Place chicken in a broiling pan and arrange skin side down; sprinkle with rosemary and paprika. Broil in a preheated broiler for 10 minutes; turn and sprinkle with additional paprika, if desired. Broil 10 minues more or until cooked through. Makes 4 servings.

Chicken Fruit Skillet

2 tablespoons unsalted butter or margarine
2 whole chicken breasts, boned, skinned, and cut into
    1½-inch chunks
¼ cup chopped onion
¼ teaspoon dried leaf tarragon
⅛ teaspoon pepper
¼ cup orange juice
½ cup dark grapes, halved and seeded
2 bananas

Melt butter in a large skillet. Add chicken chunks and cook over moderately high heat until white, stirring frequently. Add onion and cook 1 minute; add tarragon and pepper and stir in orange juice. Cover and cook 15 minutes. Stir in grapes. Peel and slice bananas; add to chicken and heat through. Makes 4 servings.

Flounder Florentine

4 thin slices fillet of flounder
1 10-ounce package frozen chopped spinach, thawed
1 tablespoon grated onion
¼ teaspoon nutmeg
1 tablespoon unsalted butter
¼ cup lemon juice
1 tablespoon chopped dill

Preheat oven to 350°F. Cut each slice of fish in half lengthwise. Combine spinach, onion, and nutmeg; spread on fish slices and roll up jelly-roll fashion. Fasten with toothpicks and place in a buttered baking dish. Heat butter in a small saucepan; add lemon juice and dill. Spoon over fish and bake, uncovered, about 25 minutes, or until fish flakes easily. Makes 4 servings

Baked Cod Fillets

2 tablespoons salad oil
2 pounds cod fillets
½ teaspoon paprika
2 tablespoons unsalted butter
1 small onion, diced
1 small clove garlic, minced
3 tomatoes, cut up
½ cup dry white wine
1 teaspoon sugar
⅛ teaspoon pepper

Preheat oven to 350°F. Paint salad oil over all sides of cod fillets; arrange in one layer in a baking dish and sprinkle with paprika. Melt butter in a small saucepan; sauté onion and garlic for several minutes. Add tomatoes, wine, sugar, and pepper; stir and simmer for several minutes. Pour sauce over fish and bake about 30 minutes, or until fish flakes easily. Makes 4 servings.

Sweet and Sour Whitefish

2 large onions, sliced
2 cups water
½ cup tarragon vinegar
½ cup sugar
1 teaspoon ground ginger
½ teaspoon pepper
3 pounds whitefish steaks

Heat onions and water in a heavy saucepan; simmer 10 minutes. Add vinegar, sugar, ginger, and pepper and simmer 5 minutes more. Remove from heat. Place fish steaks in onion-water mixture and marinate about 10 minutes, adding more water if necessary to cover fish. Then bring mixture to a boil; reduce heat and simmer 35 to 45 minutes, covered, or until fish flakes easily, adding additional water if necessary to keep fish covered. Makes 4 to 6 servings.

Broiled Salmon Steaks

4 salmon steaks, about 1 inch thick
½ cup salad oil
¼ teaspoon tarragon
⅛ teaspoon pepper
2 tablespoons melted unsalted butter
Lemon slices
Parsley

Combine salad oil, tarragon, and pepper. Wipe steaks dry and marinate in oil at least one hour at room temperature. Drain and broil in a preheated broiler at least 20 minutes, basting frequently with melted butter. Serve with lemon slices and parsley. Makes 4 servings.

Mousse au Chocolat

2 ounces baking chocolate
3 tablespoons sugar
3 tablespoons boiling water
1 teaspoon rum
2 eggs, separated

Grate chocolate and place in an electric blender; add sugar and boiling water and blend. Add rum and egg yolks; blend again. Beat egg whites until stiff and fold in chocolate mixture. Spoon into dessert dishes and chill until firm. Makes 4 servings.

Orange Sherbet

2 eggs
½ cup sugar
½ cup light corn syrup
2 cups buttermilk
1 6-ounce can frozen orange juice concentrate, thawed
¼ teaspoon grated orange rind

Beat eggs in a large bowl. Slowly beat in sugar, then corn syrup; mix in buttermilk, orange juice concentrate, and rind. Pour into metal pan and place in freezer; freeze until almost firm, about 1 hour. Turn into a large mixer bowl, break up into small pieces, and beat smooth. Return to freezer pan or serving dishes and freeze until firm, about 3 hours. Makes 1 quart sherbet.

12

The Low-Purine Diet

The Low-Purine diet is generally prescribed for sufferers of gout, to be followed between attacks during periods of remission. When acute attacks occur, a stricter form of the Low-Purine diet is usually recommended, omitting all meat, fowl, and fish until the attack subsides. Whether you follow the regular or the strict version of this diet, it's important to avoid excessive use of fats; also, don't serve organ meats like liver, kidneys, and sweetbreads. Dried peas and beans are forbidden.

Be sure to plan menus with this limitation of protein-rich foods in mind, and serve extra helpings of milk, eggs, and cheese to make it up. Check with your doctor or hospital dietician to find out if skim milk would be a better choice than regular whole milk.

Aside from its limited protein, this diet offers a good variety of nutritious foods, so vitamin supplements may not be necessary.

	FOODS ALLOWED	**FOODS TO OMIT**
Beverages:	Decaffeinated coffee; milk, skim milk, buttermilk—include 3 cups daily in some form. Carbonated beverages.	Coffee, tea, cocoa, and alcoholic beverages.
Eggs:	All kinds, except fried—include 2 daily to supply protein.	Fried eggs.
Fats:	Butter, margarine, cream, and oil in moderation. If restricted, limit to 1 tablespoon of fat daily.	Fried foods, gravy; excessive butter, cream, etc.
Cheese:	All cheese—include at least 2 ounces daily to supply protein. Cheddar and cream cheese should be limited to 2 ounces if diet is very restricted.	None, except those with nuts or spices.
Breads and cereals:	Enriched white bread, rolls, biscuits, muffins, crackers. Refined hot cereals such as cream of wheat, farina, cornmeal, rice cereals, and corn cereals; dry rice and corn cereals.	Whole-grain bread and muffins, doughnuts, crackers, pancakes, waffles, rich breads, oatmeal, whole-grain cereals.

Vegetables:	Beets, broccoli, brussels sprouts, carrots, cabbage, celery, corn, eggplant, leeks, lettuce, onions, okra, string beans, squash, tomatoes, and wax beans.	Asparagus, cauliflower, peas, mushrooms, peppers, spinach, dried beans, dried peas, and lentils.
Fruits:	All—include 1 serving of citrus or juice daily.	None.
Potato or substitutes:	White potato, sweet potato; macaroni, spaghetti, noodles, rice.	Fried potatoes, potato chips, spicy sauces on pasta.
Soup:	Cream soups made with permitted vegetables.	Broth soups, meat stock soups, bouillon; dried beans, dried peas, or lentil soups.
Meat, fish and poultry:	Lean meats, fish, and poultry—2 servings daily unless restricted to protein substitutes such as eggs, cheese, creamy peanut butter.	Organ meats, gravy, wild game, duck, goose, anchovies, herring, sardines, mackerel, shrimp, scallops, oysters.
Desserts:	Plain, simple desserts; fruit-flavored gelatin, ice cream, plain cake, puddings.	Rich desserts, pastries, mincemeat, chocolate, nuts, and all high-fat-content desserts

Miscellaneous: Sugar, honey, jelly, jam, gumdrops, hard candies, salt, mild herbs, vinegar, creamy peanut butter. Condiments, pepper, spices, sauces, fried foods, pickles, yeast, nuts, cocoa, and chocolate.

SUGGESTED MENU PLAN

Breakfast
Citrus fruit or juice
Cereal with milk
White toast
Butter
Jelly
Hot beverage
Milk

Lunch
Cream Soup
Cheese or egg dish
Vegetable
Salad
White bread
Butter
Jelly
Fruit
Milk

Dinner
Meat, fish, or fowl (or substitute egg or cheese dish)
Potato or substitute
Vegetable
Bread
Butter
Jelly
Dessert
Milk

RECIPES

In addition to these recipes for a Low-Purine Diet, the following recipes may also be used:

Beverages:

Eggs:

Vegetables:

Poultry:
Apricot Jellied Turkey Roll   64
Baked Chicken and Apricots 103
Baked Chicken with Peaches   80
Baked Chicken with Pineapple-Cheese Sauce 237
Baked Orange Chicken   43
Broiled Tarragon Chicken   82
Chicken Stroganoff 123
Chicken Tetrazzini 124
Peachy Broiled Chicken 103
Roast Turkey 64

Fish:
Boiled Fish 104
Broiled Haddock   65
Broiled Lemon Flounder   43
Poached Fish Rolls   65
Poached Haddock 126
Tuna Cheese Casserole 126
Tuna Lasagna 127

Desserts:
Angel Food Cake 66
Baked Rice Pudding 107
Bread Pudding Meringue 84
Caramel Pudding 241
Cheese Cake 246
Coffee Custard 84
Cupcakes 248
Gelatin Parfait 106
Orange Sponge Cake 85
Peachy Gelatin 45

Peanut Butter Cookies 249
  (use creamy peanut butter)
Prune Whip 105
Rice Cream 106
Soft Custard 22
Sponge Cake 245
Sugar Cookies 85
Vanilla Cookies 48
Vanilla Pudding 241

Spanish Omelet

1 small onion, sliced thin
1 stalk celery, sliced thin
½ green pepper, seeded and sliced thin
1 cup canned tomatoes, with juice
3 eggs
1 tablespoon water
¼ teaspoon salt
1 tablespoon butter

Combine onion, celery, green pepper, and tomatoes in a small saucepan; simmer until onion and celery are soft. Beat eggs and water; add salt. Heat butter in a large skillet and pour in eggs. With a spatula or fork, carefully draw the cooked portion toward the center so the uncooked portion flows to the bottom; slide pan rapidly back and forth over heat to keep mixture in motion. When eggs are set, slide omelet onto a plate. Fill with hot tomato mixture and fold over. Serve at once. Makes 1 or 2 servings.

Broccoli Milk Soup

1 10-ounce package frozen broccoli, *or*
½ pound fresh broccoli
2 cups milk or skim milk
1 tablespoon farina
¼ teaspoon dried dillweed
¼ teaspoon salt

Cook broccoli in a small amount of water until soft. Drain. Place in an electric blender with 1 cup milk and blend until smooth. Pour into a small saucepan; add remaining milk, farina, dill, and salt. Simmer and stir until mixture is hot and slightly thickened. Makes 4 servings.

Celery Milk Soup

2 cups diced celery
½ teaspoon salt
½ cup water
2 cups milk or skim milk
1 tablespoon farina
1 teaspoon butter
½ teaspoon sugar
¼ teaspoon marjoram

Simmer diced celery in salted water until tender. Pour into an electric blender and blend until smooth; add 1 cup milk and blend again. Pour into a saucepan; add remaining milk, farina, butter, sugar, and marjoram. Simmer and stir until hot and slightly thickened. Makes 4 servings.

Cold Borscht

1 1-pound can sliced beets, with juice
1 cup water
1 tablespoon lemon juice
1 teaspoon sugar
¼ teaspoon salt

In an electric blender, blend beets and juice until smooth. Add water, lemon juice, sugar, and salt; blend again. Chill. Makes 6 servings.

Cabbage Soup

½ small head of cabbage, shredded
1 2-pound can tomatoes
1 quart water
1 apple, peeled and diced
2 tablespoons brown sugar
3 tablespoons lemon juice
¾ teaspoon salt

Place cabbage and tomatoes in a deep saucepan; add water, apple, sugar, lemon juice, and salt. Simmer, covered, 2 hours. Makes 6 servings.

Potato Soup

4 large peeled potatoes, diced
1 onion, diced fine
2 stalks celery, diced fine
2 cups water
2 cups milk or skim milk
½ teaspoon dried dillweed
½ teaspoon salt
1 teaspoon butter
Chopped chives

Place potatoes, onion, celery, water, and milk in a saucepan; add dill, salt, and butter. Simmer 20 minutes, or until potatoes are soft. Ladle into bowls and top with chopped chives. Makes 6 servings.

Broccoli Cheddar Bake

2 10-ounce packages frozen broccoli stalks
¼ teaspoon salt
½ cup mayonnaise
¼ cup grated cheddar cheese
1 teaspoon grated onion
1 teaspoon lemon juice
2 hard-cooked eggs, sliced

Preheat oven to 350°F. Place broccoli in a saucepan with salt and enough water to cover. Cook 15 minutes, or until tender; drain. Place in a greased casserole. Combine mayonnaise, cheese, onion, and lemon juice; spread half the mixture over the broccoli. Arrange hard-cooked egg slices in a single layer on broccoli and top with remaining cheese mixture. Bake 25 minutes. Makes 4 servings.

Brussels Sprouts

1 quart fresh brussels sprouts
½ teaspoon salt
½ teaspoon dried dillweed
3 tablespoons butter or margarine

Wash brussels sprouts thoroughly. Place in a saucepan and cover with water; add salt and dill. Cook 10 to 15 minutes, or until very tender. Drain, toss with butter, and serve. Makes 6 servings.

Eggplant Parmesan

1 eggplant, peeled and sliced thin
Salt
2 cups tomato juice
2 tablespoons tomato paste
1 teaspoon sugar
½ teaspoon salt
½ teaspoon oregano
1 pound sliced mozzarella cheese
½ cup grated Parmesan cheese

Dust each slice of eggplant lightly with salt. Pile slices on top of each other, weight with a plate, and let stand at room temperature at least 30 minutes. Pat dry with paper towels. Preheat oven to 350° F. Combine tomato juice, tomato paste, sugar, salt, and oregano. Grease a large flat baking dish. Spoon some of the tomato sauce into a thin layer in the baking dish; cover with slices of eggplant, top with a layer of sliced mozzarella cheese, and sprinkle with grated Parmesan cheese. Repeat layers of sauce, eggplant, and cheese, finishing with at least two layers topped with cheese. Bake 35 minutes, or until eggplant is fork-tender. Makes 6 servings.

Stuffed Eggplant

2 medium eggplants
1 onion, diced
4 stalks celery, diced
1 cup tomato juice
½ teaspoon salt
½ teaspoon oregano
1 egg
1 cup cornflake crumbs
½ cup grated Parmesan cheese

Cut eggplants in half and scoop out flesh carefully, leaving unbroken shells. Dice scooped-out-eggplant; place in a saucepan with celery, tomato juice, salt, and oregano and simmer until soft. Remove from heat. Preheat oven to 350° F. Add egg and cornflake crumbs to mixture in saucepan and stir in half the cheese. Fill eggplant shells with this mixture; sprinkle with remaining cheese. Bake 20 minutes. Makes 4 servings.

Red Cabbage

1 medium red cabbage
1 cup boiling water
2 onions, sliced thin
2 large apples, peeled and sliced thin
2 tablespoons lemon juice
1 tablespoon sugar
½ teaspoon salt

Shred cabbage and place in a large saucepan. Pour boiling water over cabbage; add onions, apples, lemon juice, sugar, and salt. Bring to a boil, then reduce heat and simmer about 20 minutes, or until cabbage is soft. Makes 6 servings.

Broiled Tomatoes

4 medium tomatoes
2 tablespoons white bread crumbs
2 teaspoons butter
¼ teaspoon oregano

Cut each tomato in half and place cut side up in a shallow pan. Top with bread crumbs and dot with butter; sprinkle with oregano. Broil in a preheated broiler 8 minutes, or until browned and bubbly. Makes 8 servings.

Zucchini

1 16-ounce can whole tomatoes
2 large zucchini, sliced thick
4 stalks celery, sliced thin
1 medium onion, sliced thin
¼ teaspoon salt
¼ teaspoon ground thyme

Empty tomatoes into a saucepan and break up with a spoon. Add zucchini, celery, onion, salt, and thyme. Cover and simmer 15 minutes, stirring occasionally, until vegetables are tender. Makes 6 servings.

Parsleyed Potatoes

1 pound tiny new potatoes
¼ teaspoon salt
¼ cup butter
¼ cup minced parsley
2 teaspoons lemon juice

Wash potatoes, leaving skins intact. Cover with water and add salt; boil 10 to 15 minutes, or until fork-tender. In a small saucepan, melt butter; add parsley and lemon juice. Peel potatoes quickly and place in a serving bowl; pour melted butter over potatoes and toss lightly. Serve at once. Makes 4 servings.

Baked Stuffed Potatoes Parmesan

4 baking potatoes
⅓ cup milk
1 tablespoon butter
½ teaspoon salt
¼ cup Parmesan cheese

Preheat oven to 350°F. Wash potatoes and bake 1 hour, or until fork-tender. Cut in half lengthwise; scoop out insides and reserve skins. Mash potatoes; add milk, butter, and salt and beat until fluffy. Spoon mixture back into potato shells and top with a heavy sprinkling of Parmesan cheese. Place on a baking sheet and return to oven for 20 minutes, or until tops are lightly browned. Serve at once. Makes 8 servings.

NOTE: These potatoes can be prepared earlier and refrigerated until 30 minutes before mealtime; then proceed with the second baking. They can also be prepared and frozen for future use—to reheat, bake 30 minutes, no thawing necessary.

Noodle Pudding Parmesan

1 12-ounce package broad egg noodles
½ teaspoon salt
1 quart water
2 cups crushed corn flakes
1 cup grated Parmesan cheese
¼ cup soft butter
2 tablespoons finely chopped parsley

Preheat oven to 350°F. Cook noodles in boiling salted water for 8 minutes; drain thoroughly. Combine corn flake crumbs and cheese and add to noodles. Add butter and parsley and toss lightly. Spoon into a buttered casserole and bake for 15 minutes. Makes 6 servings.

Stuffed Baked Manicotti

1 1-pound package manicotti
1 pound ricotta cheese
3 tablespoons Parmesan cheese
½ teaspoon salt
1 1-pound can tomatoes
2 tablespoons tomato paste
½ cup Italian-seasoned bread crumbs

Cook manicotti according to package directions; remove from water as soon as pasta is pliable. Combine cheeses and salt; stuff noodle tubes with the mixture and place side by side in a greased flat casserole. Preheat oven to 350° F. Blend tomatoes and tomato paste in an electric blender; spoon over stuffed manicotti and top with bread crumbs. Bake 30 minutes. Makes 4 to 6 servings.

Baked Veal Chops

4 veal chops, ¾ inch thick
¼ cup tomato juice
½ cup crushed corn flakes
4 slices lemon

Preheat oven to 375°F. Dip chops in tomato juice and then into crushed corn flakes; place in an ungreased shallow baking pan. Bake 45 minutes, or until fork-tender. Serve with lemon slices. Makes 4 servings.

Peachy Baked Chicken

1 broiler chicken, quartered
½ cup milk
¼ cup flour
½ teaspoon salt
1 1-pound can peach halves, with syrup

Preheat oven to 375°F. Dip chicken in milk and then in flour mixed with salt; place in a shallow baking dish and bake 30 minutes. Drain syrup from peaches; reserve ½ cup syrup. Place peach halves around chicken and spoon reserved syrup over chicken and peaches. Bake 20 minutes longer. Makes 4 servings.

Orange Glazed Chicken

1 broiler chicken, quartered
½ cup frozen orange juice concentrate
⅓ cup sugar
½ teaspoon thyme
½ teaspoon salt
½ cup water
1 teaspoon cornstarch

Preheat oven to 350°F. Arrange chicken in a shallow baking pan. Combine orange juice concentrate, sugar, thyme, salt, water, and cornstarch in a small saucepan; heat and stir until smooth and thick. Pour over chicken and bake 1 hour. Makes 4 servings.

13

The Gluten-Free Diet

There are times when a troubled tummy can be traced to a sensitivity to all gluten products. This means that all forms of wheat, rye, buckwheat, and barley have to be eliminated from the diet, except for a gluten-free wheat starch that can be obtained in special health stores. Don't despair — rice, corn, potato flour, and soybean are used instead, producing very tasty results.

Be sure to read food labels very carefully to make sure they don't include any of the forbidden gluten products. Anything with gluten in it will cause an immediate eruption of the trouble.

Aside from the grains that must be eliminated from your diet or your patient's, all other foods are permitted. This should provide good nutrition, so further vitamin supplements are not necessary if your menu is planned carefully.

	FOODS ALLOWED	**FOODS TO OMIT**
Beverages:	Milk, cocoa (if no wheat flour has been added—read label), coffee (made from ground coffee only), tea, carbonated beverages, wine, and brandy.	Cereal beverages, malted milk, Ovaltine, beer, ale, and all liquors made from forbidden grains.
Eggs:	All kinds, except those stirred up with wheat flour—include 1 or 2 a day.	No omelets or soufflés made with wheat flour.
Fats:	Butter, margarine, and other fats and oils as desired.	Cream sauces made with wheat flour, commercial salad dressings that contain wheat products—read label.
Cheese:	Cottage cheese, cream cheese, and bacteria-ripened cheeses.	Processed cheeses.

Breads and cereals:	Bread, rolls, muffins, cakes, and cookies made with rice, corn, soybean, or potato flour and gluten-free wheat starch. Hominy, rice, and corn cereals.	All bread, rolls, muffins, crackers, biscuits, waffles, pancakes, etc. made with wheat, rye, or oats. All prepared mixes and breaded foods; wheat, rye, and oat cereals, wheat germ, barley, buckwheat, and kasha.
Vegetables:	All except creamed or sauced made with wheat flour.	Only those prepared with cream sauce or breaded, containing omitted grains.
Fruit:	All.	None.
Potato and substitutes:	Potatoes or rice.	All pasta, dumplings, and cream sauces made from wheat flour.
Soup:	All clear and vegetable soups; cream soups thickened with cornstarch, rice, or potato flour only.	All canned soups except clear broth, all cream soups thickened with wheat flour.

Meat, fish, and poultry:	All kinds, except those prepared with bread crumbs, or stuffings, or cold cuts made with cereal fillers.	Breaded meat, patties and meat loaves made with regular bread crumbs, canned meats with fillers (read labels) and cold cuts made with fillers; stuffings made with bread; gravy made with wheat flour.
Desserts:	Fruit-flavored gelatin, fruit ice, sherbet, homemade ice cream, custard, rennet puddings, rice pudding, homemade cornstarch puddings.	Cakes, cookies, pastry, commercial ice cream, prepared mixes, puddings made with wheat flour.
Miscellaneous:	Salt, herbs, spices, chocolate, sugar, honey, jelly, jam, gumdrops, hard candy, marshmallows, plain mints.	Commercial candies containing cereal products. Anything containing wheat, rye, or oat flour.

SUGGESTED MENU PLAN

Breakfast
Fruit juice
Allowed cereal with milk
Egg
Bread substitute
Butter
Beverage
Cream
Sugar

Lunch
Clear broth
Meat, fish, or poultry
Vegetable
Salad
Bread substitute
Butter
Fruit or dessert
Milk

Dinner
Fruit juice
Meat, fish, or poultry
Potato or rice
Vegetable
Bread substitute
Butter
Dessert
Milk

RECIPES

In addition to these recipes for a Gluten-Free Diet, the following recipes may also be used:

Beverages:
    Eggnog 19
    Double Milk Eggnog 54
    Orange Eggnog 19
    Slim Skimnog 54

Fish:

Desserts:

Substitutions

To convert your regular flour-based recipes into gluten-free recipes, try the following substitutions.

First add 1 egg to the recipe if it contains less than 2 cups of regular flour.

Then make one of the following substitutions for each cup of regular flour in the recipe:

1 cup corn flour
¾ cup coarse cornmeal
1 scant cup fine cornmeal
⅝ cup potato flour
⅞ cup rice flour
1 cup soybean flour plus ¼ cup potato flour

Cheese Soufflé

2 tablespoons butter or margarine
⅔ cup Cornstarch White Sauce Mix (see index)
1 cup water
½ pound cheddar cheese, diced
4 eggs, separated

Preheat oven to 350°F. Melt butter in a small saucepan over low heat; remove from heat and stir in White Sauce Mix and water. Bring to a boil over medium heat, stirring constantly; boil 1 minute and add cheese. Cook over medium-low heat, stirring constantly, until cheese is melted; remove from heat. In a small bowl, beat egg yolks slightly; gradually add hot cheese mixture to egg yolks, mixing well. In a large bowl, beat egg whites until stiff. Gently fold in cheese mixture. Pour into an ungreased 1½-quart soufflé dish. Place dish in a baking pan and fill with an inch of warm water. Bake 1¼ hours, or until knife inserted halfway between center and edge comes out clean. Makes 4 servings.

Spinach Soufflé

2 tablespoons grated Parmesan cheese
1 10-ounce package frozen whole-leaf spinach
1 cup milk
¼ cup cornstarch
¼ cup butter or margarine
4 eggs, separated
½ teaspoon salt
¼ teaspoon pepper
⅛ teaspoon nutmeg
Dash salt

Preheat oven to 350° F. Grease a 5-cup soufflé dish; sprinkle with grated cheese and set aside. Cook spinach; drain thoroughly, pressing out excess liquid. Chop fine. In a small saucepan, mix milk and cornstarch until smooth. Cook over medium heat, stirring constantly, until mixture comes to a boil; boil 1 minute. Remove from heat and stir in margarine (mixture may look curdled). Gradually stir in egg yolks, then spinach, salt, pepper, and nutmeg. Beat egg whites with a dash of salt until stiff peaks form; fold spinach mixture into egg whites. Spoon into prepared soufflé dish and place in a baking pan filled with 1 inch of boiling water. Bake 40 to 45 minutes, or until knife inserted in center comes out clean. Makes 4 to 6 servings.

Cream of Lettuce Soup

4 cups iceberg lettuce, shredded, packed well
2 chicken bouillon cubes, crumbled
¾ cup water
2 tablespoons lemon juice
2 tablespoons butter or margarine
1 medium onion, sliced into rings
2 tablespoons cornstarch
½ teaspoon salt
¼ teaspoon white pepper
Dash nutmeg
2 cups milk
¼ cup white wine, *or*
  3 tablespoons water and 1 tablespoon lemon juice

Blend lettuce, bouillon cubes, water, and lemon juice in
electric blender until smooth. In a saucepan, melt butter over
medium heat. Add onion rings and sauté until tender but not
brown; remove from pan. In remaining butter in pan, blend
cornstarch, salt, pepper, and nutmeg. Remove from heat and
gradually stir in milk. Cook over medium heat, stirring
constantly, until mixture comes to a boil; boil 1 minute. Stir in
lettuce mixture and wine; add onion and heat to serving
temperature. Makes 4 servings.

Cream of Asparagus Soup

¼ cup butter or margarine
⅔ cup Cornstarch White Sauce Mix (see index)
1 chicken bouillon cube
2 cups water
1 cup cooked asparagus, chopped fine

Melt butter in a saucepan over low heat. Remove from heat; add White Sauce Mix, bouillon cube, and water. Bring to a boil over medium heat, stirring constantly; boil 1 minute, stir in asparagus, and heat thoroughly. Makes 4 servings.

NOTE: For variety, substitute any other cooked vegetable for the asparagus, and prepare as above.

Harvard Beets #2

½ cup sugar
1 tablespoon cornstarch
½ teaspoon grated lemon rind
⅓ cup lemon juice
⅓ cup water
3 cups cooked beets (about 2 pounds fresh beets), *or*
   2 1-pound cans sliced beets, with liquid

In a saucepan, mix sugar, cornstarch, lemon rind and juice, and water; substitute beet liquid for water if using canned beets. Bring to a boil, stirring constantly; boil 1 minute. Add sliced beets to sauce and simmer 15 minutes, stirring occasionally. Makes 6 servings.

Cauliflower Casserole

1 medium head cauliflower, cleaned
  and broken into flowerets
2 tablespoons butter or margarine
1 tablespoon cornstarch
¼ teaspoon dried rosemary
¼ teaspoon dried tarragon
1 cup milk
½ cup grated Swiss cheese
1 egg yolk, slightly beaten

Preheat oven to 400°F. Cook cauliflower in boiling salted water about 12 minutes, until tender-crisp. Drain, reserving ½ cup liquid, and place in a 1-quart casserole. Meanwhile, melt butter in a small saucepan over medium heat. Stir in cornstarch, rosemary, and tarragon. Remove from heat. Gradually add milk, stirring until smooth; mix in reserved liquid and ¼ cup cheese. Cook over medium heat, stirring constantly, until cheese melts. Mix a little hot mixture into egg yolk, then stir into remaining hot mixture in saucepan. Cook, stirring constantly, about 1 minute; do not let mixture boil. Pour over cauliflower, sprinkle with remaining cheese, and bake about 10 minutes or until hot. Makes 4 to 6 servings.

Cornstarch White Sauce Mix

2¾ cups instant nonfat dry milk
½ cup cornstarch
1 teaspoon salt
½ teaspoon pepper

Stir all ingredients together; store in a tightly covered jar at room temperature. Makes 2⅔ cups mix.

NOTE: Stir White Sauce Mix before each use.

Medium White Sauce

2 tablespoons butter or margarine
⅓ cup Cornstarch White Sauce Mix (see index)
¾ cup water

Melt butter in a small saucepan over low heat. Remove from heat and stir in White Sauce Mix and water. Bring to a boil over medium heat, stirring constantly; boil 1 minute. Makes about 1 cup sauce.

NOTE: For Thin White Sauce: Use ⅓ cup White Sauce Mix and 1 cup water, following directions above.
For Thick White Sauce: Use ⅔ cup White Sauce Mix and 1 cup water, following directions above.

Creamed Vegetables

2 tablespoons butter or margarine
⅓ cup Cornstarch White Sauce Mix (see index)
¾ cup water
3 cups cooked vegetables

Melt butter in a saucepan over low heat. Remove from heat and stir in White Sauce Mix and water. Bring to a boil over medium heat, stirring constantly; boil 1 minute and add hot cooked vegetables. Makes 6 servings.

Potato Puff

2 cups cooked mashed potatoes
1 cup cottage cheese
½ cup dairy sour cream
2 tablespoons chopped chives
½ teaspoon salt
⅛ teaspoon pepper
3 eggs, separated

Preheat oven to 350°F. Combine mashed potatoes, cottage cheese, sour cream, chives, salt, and pepper. Beat egg yolks slightly and add to mixture. Beat egg whites until stiff peaks form; fold through potato mixture. Spoon into a greased 2-quart casserole and bake 50 minutes. Makes 8 servings.

Hot Potato Salad

6 medium potatoes
⅓ cup chopped green onion
2 stalks celery, thinly sliced
6 slices bacon
1 tablespoon cornstarch
½ cup cider vinegar
½ cup water
2 tablespoons light corn syrup
½ teaspoon paprika
½ teaspoon salt
½ teaspoon dry mustard
¼ teaspoon pepper
1 tablespoon chopped parsley

Cook potatoes in boiling water in a covered saucepan until tender. Peel and slice thin; sprinkle with onion and celery. Cook bacon until crisp; drain, crumble, and add to potatoes. Blend cornstarch with bacon drippings in skillet; do not brown. Stir in vinegar, water, corn syrup, paprika, salt, dry mustard, and pepper. Simmer 8 to 10 minutes, or until slightly thickened. Pour over potatoes, toss gently, and sprinkle with parsley. Let stand about 1 hour at room temperature before serving, to blend flavors. Makes 6 servings.

Rice with Spicy Tomato Sauce

1 14-ounce can stewed tomatoes, with liquid
1 3-ounce can sliced mushrooms, with liquid
2 tablespoons cornstarch
¼ teaspoon salt
¼ teaspoon dried basil
Dash Worcestershire sauce
3 cups cooked rice

Combine stewed tomatoes and mushrooms, with liquid, in a saucepan. Stir in cornstarch, salt, and basil; add a dash of Worcestershire sauce. Bring to a boil, stirring constantly; boil 1 minute. Serve over hot cooked rice. Makes 1⅔ cups sauce and serves 6.

NOTE: This spicy tomato sauce may also be served over fish cakes or meat loaf.

Swedish Meatballs

1 pound ground beef
½ pound ground pork or veal
1 egg
1 cup prepared mashed potatoes
2 tablespoons grated onion
1 teaspoon salt
1 teaspoon sugar
¼ teaspoon pepper
¼ teaspoon nutmeg
⅛ teaspoon ginger
¼ cup butter

Combine ground beef, ground pork or veal, and egg; add mashed potatoes, onion, salt, sugar, pepper, nutmeg, and ginger and mix thoroughly. Form into 1-inch balls. Melt butter in a large skillet; brown meatballs over low heat, shaking pan occasionally to brown on all sides. Makes about 4 dozen meatballs.

Baked Swiss Steak

¾ pound round steak (about ¾ inch thick)
2 tablespoons potato flour
½ teaspoon salt
⅛ teaspoon pepper
2 slices bacon
1 16-ounce can tomatoes
1 onion, sliced
2 stalks celery, sliced
2 carrots, scraped and sliced
¼ teaspoon Worcestershire sauce

Preheat oven to 350°F. Dust round steak with potato flour, salt, and pepper. Cook bacon in a skillet until crisp; remove and drain. Brown meat on both sides in hot bacon fat and transfer to a flat baking dish. Combine tomatoes, onion, celery, carrots, and Worcestershire sauce in the same skillet; heat until mixture boils, stirring constantly. Pour tomato mixture over meat and sprinkle with crumbled bacon. Cover tightly and bake 1½ hours or until meat is fork-tender, adding water if necessary. Makes 2 to 3 servings.

Baked Chicken with
Pineapple-Cheese Sauce

1 frying chicken, cut up
1 teaspoon salt
¼ teaspoon pepper
¼ teaspoon ground thyme
3 tablespoons butter
1 8¾-ounce can pineapple tidbits, with juice
½ cup shredded cheddar cheese

Preheat oven to 350°F. Arrange chicken pieces in a buttered flat baking dish. Sprinkle with salt, pepper, and thyme and dot with butter. Pour pineapple and juice over chicken. Bake 40 minutes; top with shredded cheese and bake an additional 10 minutes, or until cheese is melted. Makes 4 servings.

Oriental Fried Chicken

½ cup dark corn syrup
½ cup soy sauce
¼ cup rice wine or sweet white wine
3 whole chicken breasts, skinned, boned,
     and cut in bite-sized pieces
¾ cup cornstarch
2 cups corn oil

Mix corn syrup, soy sauce, and wine; pour over chicken pieces and marinate 1 hour in the refrigerator. Drain well on paper towels. Place cornstarch in a large bag; add chicken a small amount at a time and shake to coat evenly. Heat corn oil over medium heat in a deep skillet; fry coated chicken pieces in oil about 1 minute, or until both sides are golden brown. Drain and serve immediately. Makes 6 servings, or may be served as an appetizer.

Chicken on Rice

2 frying chickens, cut up
2 cups sliced celery stalks and leaves
¾ cup fresh parsley
2 medium onions, sliced
1 chicken bouillon cube
2 teaspoons salt
1 bay leaf
¼ teaspoon thyme
6 tablespoons cornstarch
4 cups cooked rice

Place chicken in a 6-quart kettle; cover with water and add celery, parsley, onions, bouillon cube, salt, bay leaf, and thyme. Cover; bring to a boil and then reduce heat and simmer 1¼ hours, or until chicken is tender. Remove chicken and discard bones. Strain broth; measure 6 cups, adding boiling water if necessary. Return 5 cups broth to kettle; mix together remaining broth and cornstarch until smooth and stir into broth in the kettle. Bring to a boil, stirring constantly, and boil 1 minute, until mixture is slightly thickened. Add chicken and heat. Serve over rice in soup bowls. Makes 8 servings.

Blueberry-Rice Muffins

1½ cups rice flour
⅔ cup hot water
2 tablespoons vegetable shortening
¼ cup sugar
3 tablespoons baking powder
¼ teaspoon salt
1 teaspoon vanilla
1 teaspoon grated lemon rind
½ cup fresh blueberries, washed, stems removed

Preheat oven to 375°F. Combine half the flour with hot water; set aside. Cream together shortening and sugar; add flour mixture and beat well. Stir together remaining flour, sugar, baking powder, and salt, and add flour mixture, vanilla, and grated lemon rind to batter. Stir in blueberries. Spoon into a greased muffin tin and bake 20 minutes. Makes 8 muffins.

Rye Bread

2 cups rye flour
2 tablespoons sugar
3 tablespoons baking powder
½ teaspoon salt
½ cup water
2 teaspoons corn oil

Preheat oven to 350°F. Sift together rye flour, sugar, baking powder, and salt; add water and oil and beat thoroughly. Pour into a greased loaf pan and bake 40 minutes, or until lightly browned. Makes 1 loaf.

Corn Bread

2 cups corn flour
3 tablespoons baking powder
2 tablespoons sugar
½ teaspoon salt
½ cup water
2 teaspoons corn oil

Preheat oven to 350°F. Sift together corn flour, baking powder, sugar, and salt. Add water and oil and beat thoroughly. Pour into a greased loaf pan and bake 40 minutes, or until lightly browned. Makes 1 loaf.

Blancmange

½ cup sugar
5 tablespoons cornstarch
¼ teaspoon salt
4 cups milk
1½ teaspoons vanilla

Mix sugar, cornstarch, and salt in the top of a double boiler. Gradually add milk, stirring until smooth. Cook over boiling water, stirring constantly, until mixture thickens enough to mound slightly when dropped from a spoon; cover and cook 10 minutes longer, stirring occasionally. Remove from heat and stir in vanilla; pour into individual dishes and chill. Serve plain or with fresh fruit. Makes 6 to 8 servings.

Vanilla Pudding

⅓ cup sugar
¼ cup cornstarch
⅛ teaspoon salt
2¾ cups milk
2 tablespoons butter or margarine
1 teaspoon vanilla

Combine sugar, cornstarch, salt, and milk in a large saucepan; mix until smooth. Cook over medium heat, stirring constantly, until mixture comes to a boil; boil 1 minute and remove from heat. Stir in butter and vanilla and pour into individual serving dishes. Chill. Makes 6 servings.

Caramel Pudding

½ cup sugar
¼ cup water
2¾ cups milk
¼ cup cornstarch
2 tablespoons sugar
⅛ teaspoon salt
2 tablespoons butter or margarine
1 teaspoon vanilla

Heat ½ cup sugar and 2 tablespoons water in a large, heavy saucepan over medium-high heat, stirring occasionally, about 5 minutes, or until bubbly and caramel-colored. Remove from heat and carefully add remaining 2 tablespoons water; after mixture stops foaming, add 2 cups milk. Blend remaining milk, cornstarch, 2 tablespoons sugar, and salt until smooth; stir into caramel milk. Cook over medium heat, stirring constantly, until mixture comes to a boil; boil 1 minute and remove from heat. Stir in butter and vanilla and pour into individual serving dishes. Chill. Makes 6 servings.

Eggs à la Neige

2 eggs, separated
¼ teaspoon cream of tartar
½ cup sugar
1 tablespoon cornstarch
¼ teaspoon salt
2 cups light cream or milk
1 teaspoon vanilla
1 pint strawberries, hulled and sliced, *or*
  2 oranges, sectioned, and 2 bananas, sliced, *or*
   1 12-ounce can mandarin orange sections, drained,
  and 1 pound grapes, seeded.
2 tablespoons unsweetened chocolate, flaked

Beat egg whites and cream of tartar until foamy; add ¼ cup sugar and beat until stiff peaks form. Half-fill deep skillet with water; bring water almost to a boil and remove from heat. Drop meringue mixture by tablespoonfuls into water; cover 1 minute. Drain on absorbent paper and chill 1 to 2 hours. Combine remaining ¼ cup sugar, cornstarch, and salt in the top of a double boiler; mix in egg yolks and cream. Cook over boiling water, stirring constantly, 8 to 10 minutes, or until mixture is slightly thickened. Remove from boiling water and cool; stir in vanilla. Chill. Arrange fruit in the bottom of a deep serving dish; spoon custard over fruit and top with meringues. Sprinkle with flaked chocolate. Makes 4 to 6 servings.

Snow Pudding

⅓ cup sugar
¼ cup cornstarch
¼ teaspoon salt
2 cups milk
2 egg whites
1 teaspoon vanilla

Combine sugar, cornstarch, and salt in the top of a double boiler; gradually stir in milk. Cook over boiling water, stirring constantly, until mixture thickens and mounds slightly when dropped from a spoon. Cover and cook, stirring occasionally, about 20 minutes. Beat egg whites until soft peaks form; gradually fold cornstarch mixture into egg whites. Stir in vanilla. Pour into 5-ounce custard cups and chill about 2 hours, or until firm. Unmold and serve with fruit or Custard Sauce (see index). Makes 4 servings.

Custard Sauce

¼ cup sugar
1 tablespoon cornstarch
¼ teaspoon salt
1 egg, slightly beaten
2 cups milk
1 teaspoon vanilla

Combine sugar, cornstarch and salt in a 2-quart saucepan. Stir in egg and gradually add milk. Cook over medium-low heat, stirring constantly, 7 to 10 minutes, or until mixture is slightly thickened; remove from heat and stir in vanilla. Chill. Makes 2 cups sauce.

NOTE: This custard sauce can be served over baked pudding or sponge cake. Other flavorings can be substituted for vanilla as variations.

Baked Lemon Pudding

¾ cup sugar
3 tablespoons cornstarch
⅛ teaspoon salt
2 eggs, separated
1 cup milk
1 teaspoon grated lemon rind
3 tablespoons lemon juice
2 tablespoons butter or margarine, melted
¼ cup sugar

Preheat oven to 350°F. In a large bowl, sift together sugar, cornstarch, and salt. Beat egg yolks until foamy; stir in milk. Stir egg mixture gradually into dry ingredients. Add lemon rind and juice and melted butter. Beat egg whites until foamy; gradually beat in ¼ cup sugar, continuing to beat until stiff peaks form. Fold beaten egg whites into lemon mixture and spoon into a greased 1½-quart casserole. Set into a pan of hot water 1½ inches deep and bake 50 minutes, or until top is firm and well-browned. Makes 6 servings.

NOTE: Flavor can be changed to lime by substituting 1 teaspoon lime rind and 3 tablespoons lime juice for lemon rind and juice

Sponge Cake

6 eggs, separated
1 whole egg
1½ cups sugar
2 tablespoons lemon juice
Grated rind of 1 lemon
1 cup sifted potato flour
½ teaspoon salt
½ teaspoon nutmeg
Confectioners' sugar (optional)

Preheat oven to 350°F. Beat egg yolks and whole egg together until foamy; beat in sugar and add lemon juice and rind. Sift together potato flour and salt; add to egg yolk batter with nutmeg. Beat egg whites until stiff and fold into the batter. Grease bottom of 10-inch springform pan and pour batter into pan. Bake 35 minutes, or until cake is firm in center. Cool upside down before removing side of springform pan. Dust with confectioners' sugar, if desired. Makes 10 servings.

Cheese Cake

¼ cup crisp rice cereal, crushed
1 pound small curd creamed cottage cheese, as dry a
    variety as possible
2 8-ounce packages cream cheese, softened
1½ cups sugar
4 eggs, slightly beaten
⅓ cup cornstarch
2 tablespoons lemon juice
1 teaspoon vanilla
½ cup butter or margarine, melted
1 pint dairy sour cream
Fruit Glaze (optional)

Preheat oven to 325°F. Grease a 9-inch springform pan and
dust with crushed crumbs. Sieve cottage cheese into a large
mixing bowl; add cream cheese and beat at high speed until
well blended and creamy. Add sugar and beat at high speed;
add eggs and beat again. Reduce beater speed to low and add
cornstarch, lemon juice, and vanilla; beat until well blended.
Add melted butter and sour cream, beating at low speed. Pour
into prepared pan and bake 1 hour and 10 minutes, or until
firm around the edge. Turn off oven and let cake stand in oven
2 hours. Remove and cool completely on wire rack; chill. Remove side of pan. Top with Fruit Glaze, if desired. Makes about
12 servings.

Fruit Glaze:

1 tablespoon cornstarch
¼ cup cold water
⅓ cup light corn syrup
1 pint fresh berries
1 teaspoon lemon juice
Food coloring

Mix cornstarch, water, and corn syrup; add ¼ cup crushed berries. Heat to boiling and boil 1 minute. Strain. Stir in lemon juice and several drops of food coloring, red for strawberries, red and blue for blueberries, etc. Cool slightly. Arrange remaining fruit on top of Cheese Cake, spoon glaze over fruit, and chill.

Banana Bread

1 **cup rice flour**
1 **tablespoon baking powder**
½ **teaspoon salt**
¼ **cup vegetable shortening**
¼ **cup sugar**
2 **eggs, separated**
½ **cup milk**
1 **ripe banana, mashed**

Preheat oven to 325°F. Sift together rice flour, baking powder, and salt; set aside. Cream shortening; add sugar and beat until well blended. Beat in egg yolks. Add flour mixture alternately with milk, beating after each addition; add mashed banana. Beat egg whites until stiff peaks form and fold batter into egg whites. Spoon into a greased loaf pan and bake 45 minutes. Cool before slicing. Makes 1 loaf.

Cupcakes

⅓ cup butter
⅓ cup sugar
1 egg
¼ teaspoon vanilla
1 cup sifted cornstarch
1 teaspoon baking powder
3 tablespoons milk

Preheat oven to 375°F. Cream butter and sugar; add egg and vanilla. Sift together cornstarch and baking powder and add alternately with milk. Spoon batter into greased muffin tin, filling ⅔ full. Bake 12 to 15 minutes, or until an inserted toothpick comes out clean. Makes 8 servings.

Macaroons

1¼ cups ground blanched almonds
¾ cup sugar
2 egg whites
2 tablespoons cornstarch
2 teaspoons water
¼ teaspoon vanilla
Blanched almond halves

Preheat oven to 375°F. Combine ground almonds and sugar. Add unbeaten egg whites, reserving about 1 tablespoon; stir until well blended. Add cornstarch, water, and vanilla, stirring well until smooth. Drop batter by teaspoonfuls onto foil-covered baking sheet, spacing about 3 inches apart. Brush cookies with remaining egg white, then place almond half on top of each. Bake 15 minutes, or until evenly browned. Cool on wire rack 3 to 4 minutes, or until foil can be peeled off. Remove foil; cool on wire rack. Makes about 1½ dozen cookies.

Peanut Butter Cookies

1 cup creamy or chunk-style peanut butter
1 cup sugar
½ cup evaporated milk
4 teaspoons cornstarch

Preheat oven to 350°F. Stir all ingredients together and drop by teaspoonfuls onto an ungreased baking sheet. Bake 12 to 15 minutes or until light golden brown; cool 1 to 2 minutes before removing from baking sheet. Makes about 3 dozen cookies.

Coconut Pie Crust

1 3½-ounce can flaked coconut
3 tablespoons butter, melted
2 tablespoons sugar

Preheat oven to 350°F. Combine coconut, melted butter, and sugar. Press into a 9-inch pie pan and bake 15 minutes. Cool. Fill with pudding or homemade ice cream. Makes 6 servings.

Index

STRICT BLAND DIET:

REGULAR BLAND DIET:

POSTGASTRECTOMY DIET:

GLUTEN-FREE DIET: